Ice Fog, Spirit Fire and the Narrow Gate
A Journey to Constant Joy

Albert E. Hughes, M.S., M.P.M.

En Route Books & Media, LLC
St. Louis, MO

⊛*ENROUTE*
Make the time

En Route Books and Media, LLC
5705 Rhodes Avenue
St. Louis, MO 63109

Cover credit: TJ Burdick

Library of Congress Control Number:
2019943790

ISBN-13: 978-1-950108-12-1
ISBN-10: 1-950108-12-0

For

Shannon, Catherine and Martha

Dedication

To God most high, who in the name of
Jesus Christ and through the Holy Spirit,
has led me from the pit of darkness; leading
me into the valley of healing and onto the
heights of constant joy, even to exultation!
May the Triune God be worshiped and
glorified forever!

Without God, Without Any; God and
Enough Banner, Coat of Arms
Welsh Clan of Hughes

Acknowledgments

What I have become is first due to my parents, Al Sr. and Nell Hughes who, though not knowing God during my youth, still laid the foundation of a Christian social ethic and love of learning. Especially Nell Hughes, Ed.D., teacher of English and history, who was my constant mentor and advocate in my difficult teen years.

And to my beloved wife Gloria "Jeannie" McCaffrey Hughes, passed on to glory, who through constant prayer and example prepared me for conversion then, and became my walking, talking Catholic Encyclopedia in my early writing years.

And to Jesus Christ, who spoke to me, an agnostic; healed me in the flow of baptismal waters, transformed me in the Holy Spirit and gave me a mission of teaching, pastoral counseling and spiritual direction in his name.

And to Dr. Leo Stanford, Ph.D., who with his teaching staff at Seattle U. prepared me for pastoral counseling.

And to Abbot David Gaeret, Fr Ray Roh and others at the Benedictine Monastery of the Risen Christ at San Luis Obispo, CA, who prepared me for spiritual direction.

Table of Contents

Albert E. Hughes

Introduction

Dawn of Being and Purpose

Enter through the Narrow Gate; Mat 7:13

If ever I heard the whole story, how they met, I don't remember. I do know that Al, Sr., age 21, was a junior clerk at the Federal Land Bank in New Orleans, a couple of blocks off Canal Street on the Saint Charles streetcar line. He was making $40 per week in the depths of the great depression, barely a living wage in 1935. But millions had no work at all. How he met my mother-to-be is a mystery to me. She was in another state, a secretary at an obscure little factory off the southeast corner of Jackson, Mississippi. But meet, they did.

Al must have been smitten in short order. Every Friday, after work, he caught the Greyhound night run out of New Orleans and slept on that bus until the Saturday morning arrival at Jackson. That trip was not what you might think. As soon as the Greyhound passed the New Orleans airport, the concrete pavement gave way to gravel – dusty, dirty, in-your-face-open-windows dirty. (No A/C, you see?) Old highway 51 was gravel all the way to Jackson, and as far as I know, all the way to Chicago.

After a weekend of getting to know you, Sunday evening it was back on the bus night run and straight into work Monday morning; shaking the dust off his wrinkled suit. After a few months, that got old real fast. He married Nell Salter in Jackson on a rare, heavily snow-laden day; Christmas Eve, 1935. With his new bride, he made his last overnighter to New Orleans.

I made my first appearance five years later. Somebody, maybe she, later told me she had trouble conceiving. As for my part, I showed up feet first with the cord wrapped around my neck. Prophetic?

With the war on, Dad got what seemed to be his big break, promotion to management in charge of the Federal Land Bank office at the farm village of Prentiss, Mississippi. With that assignment, he needed and was allocated the last Studebaker sold in wartime New Orleans. Studebaker was too busy building tanks to produce mere automobiles. (I drove through Prentiss in '83. Prentiss looked exactly the same as in '44, 'cept the one and only street through in town, a state highway, later was paved.)

Wartime lodging was almost impossible to find. We lived in a ramshackle, loose floor board, unpainted farm tenement shack a mile of gravel west of Prentiss and sharp right up a steep red clay bank; complete with weeds, a scattering of pines, a squeaky windmill in the overgrown backyard and a rabbit infested garden near the side of the house. An abandoned gravel pit was nearby.

My earliest clear memories were of that shack, the windmill, the garden, the gravel pit, my dad's 22 rifle, and the open-cracks wooden kitchen floor upon which I played.

And I remember him taking me by the hand out by the windmill to tell me how it worked and why it squeaked; and him fussing about the rabbits that got through the chicken wire garden fence he built.

His big break quickly broke. Dad was 31 in '44, thought to be too old for it; but the draft board sent him a notice anyway: report mid-July for basic training. He was deferred for two weeks; my sister was born near the end of the month.

I remember her un-ceremonious entry into our family at a New Orleans hospital. Daddy brought the newborn out to the '42 Studebaker in an open wooden box, just barely larger than she. Gently, he placed her on the floor behind the driver's seat. Mom lay on the back seat and I rode shotgun back to Prentiss. Then, he was off to war. The three of us moved in with my maternal grandparents at Hazlehurst, Mississippi.

If loss of his job was not bad enough, he suffered basic training at Wichita Falls, Texas – in August heat! He remembered that all his life as a three-month visit to Hell. If August in Wichita Falls was not bad enough, the Army then assigned him to radio school all winter – in sub-arctic Sioux Falls, South Dakota! The following summer, for final training as a B-29 radio operator, he was assigned to his combat aircrew at Albuquerque, New Mexico – not exactly a cool summer spot on the globe, either.

Nell and I, four years old, did get to visit with him by train in '45, a winter visit to Sioux Falls followed by a summer stay at Albuquerque. One of my very early memories is of trying to walk the aisle of our coach on the famous Hiawatha of Milwaukee Railroad fame as it rocked back and forth at 103 miles per hour. (So, the conductor told us), running late from Chicago to Sioux Falls. My love of trains was well-established during that trip.

I intend not merely to share reminiscences, but also to trace how it came to be that a four-year-old boy in a sandbox became committed in mature life to a generation-long quest; seeking knowledge, wisdom and understanding of transcendent realities. Indeed, to discover an occasional dialog and a lasting relationship with the living God; accepting a God-given purpose to my life: all told in selected vignettes. Even though...

We were un-churched from the beginning; living a Christian ethic, more or less, out of the social convention of the time, not as a matter of faith and belief. I remained an agnostic until age 38, when everything changed.

My purpose is to encourage you in your search for, and response, to the fullness of Transcendent Truth. Indeed, all my published works have this intent.

"As Scripture says: *Those who instruct many in justice will shine as stars for all eternity.* They will attain this more easily if they make a covenant of perpetual obedience and strive to cling to Christ and please him alone, because, in his words, *"What you did to one of the least of my brethren, you did to me.*

Saint Joseph Calasanz, Priest. Early 17th century

+

I write with memories of the Glen Miller band playing "The Atchison, Topeka and the Santa Fe" on a front porch radio in an obscure Albuquerque neighborhood. It is mid-summer under a blazing sun – 1945.

I

The Sandbox – Kindergarten Prophecies

Aging people should know that their lives are not mounting and unfolding, but that an inexorable inner process forces the contraction of life... for the aging person it is a duty and a necessity to give serious attention to himself. After having lavished its light upon the world, the sun withdraws its rays in order to illumine itself.

Carl Gustav Jung (1875-1961)
Swiss psychologist, psychiatrist

The kindergarten in Albuquerque, New Mexico, was a long, narrow room on the back of a middle-class house, with a big back yard. In the room, there was a single line of picnic tables with benches for about 30 children, 15 on each side. The table and benches were painted blue, the walls of the room a light forest green. Wall-mounted bulletin boards displayed our best artistic works – which for the most part were pages the teacher tore out from a coloring book, colored by a crowd of four- and five-year-olds. In that room – unintended to be sure – we practiced greed and covetousness.

The basic issue was that a war was going on, both in the world and in that room. Everything was in short supply, including crayons. Each child was issued a couple of well-worn, broken crayons of random color for the day. The colors received often were unsuited to the subject of the one picture assigned at random to each child torn by the teacher from that day's coloring book. My life dream at four-and-a-half years was to have a box of crayons all my own: a box with eight, beautiful, whole crayons that no one else could use. That was not going to happen! The negotiating, bartering, argument, occasional physical emphasis and exchange of pictures and crayon bits would commence forthwith, as soon as the teacher became distracted.

It did not take long to recognize that if another child *really wanted* a green crayon which was in your possession, it might be possible to exchange for two or occasionally three crayons of other colors. This added a form of usury to the aforementioned list of greed and covetousness.

And some people deny original sin! These were near babies engaged in self-aggrandizing proto-economic warfare—traditional, cold-hearted selfishness! The mustard seed of sin. We all begin life with exclusive interest in our own wants and needs. And quite naturally so in our fallen nature.

In the face of all that, the lunch time snack, a few saltine crackers and a couple of thin slices of Hormel Spam, were welcome. There was not enough provided each child even to consider a trade. But when the temptation arose, we quickly were reminded to eat our wartime allotment: "Remember the poor starving children in China." It was not acceptable to suggest they send the

Spam to the Chinese. Nap time followed, heads down at the same table.

The climactic joy of the day was reserved for play time in the backyard. Without fail, I would run to the far left corner of the backyard to sit on a sandbox seat. The sandbox was just a bit sandier than the sunbaked dry New Mexico yard. Patches of heat seared, dry grass and thorn weeds were scattered about in the afternoon dry heat.

Dry heat? My mother would hang clothes on the backyard line of our little apartment. I held the pin bag; pins delivered on demand. They were a mixed bag of old-fashioned slotted wood pins and the new spring pins, both of which she held clenched between her teeth until needed. She worked along the line left to right, drawing clothes from a wicker basket. When done, she would go back to the beginning and remove clothes from the line in the same order as the hanging. They already were dry!

But back to the sandbox. I would sit facing away from the yard, but toward several next-door backyards, above which there was a constant flow of ascending bombers.

We were just off the end of the runway, very close to Kirtland Army Air Field. Every few minutes all day long bombers were climbing out right next to us, a hundred or so feet above us. The co-pilots of the olive drab B-17's would give us a wave through their open cockpit window as they flew by.

They were a joy to watch, but I was waiting for the B-29s. Glinting silver in their long unpainted aluminum bodies, wings spread wider than anything else on earth in their time; they were a sight to behold and I knew that my daddy was in one of them.

B-29 Bomber in Flight

You knew one was coming before you saw it. It was the tremendous roar of four huge radial engines spinning four blade props. Memory from a later time recalls those radial engines were supercharged, with two banks of nine cylinders each, the second bank offset behind the first. The prop noise was quite distinctive. Why four blades, not three like all other combat aircraft of the time?

Years later, my dad told me the story. It seems the XB-29 prototype was designed for standard props with three long blades. The first time they ran one up to full power the blades disintegrated, throwing sharp metal shards hundreds of feet. A quick math check revealed the prop tips had exceeded what was then known as "the sound barrier." The three blade props were replaced with shorter four blade props, so that the tips could not reach supersonic speeds.

Four-Blade Propellers

It was there in that sand box that the first experiential prophesy was expressed. I could not express it in words at four and a half, but the hook was set. Seventeen summers later I entered active duty as a 2nd Lieutenant in the United States Air Force.

The other prophecy was expressed in our little basement apartment where we stayed for much of that summer. I was still better than a year away from first grade when I began to express a desire for a school desk. I must have been persistent because one day I came home from kindergarten to discover a dark mahogany stained, antique wooden lift top school desk in the room where I slept. It was my great joy; then sorrow when we had to leave it there as we returned to grandma "Gommie's" house in Hazlehurst, Mississippi. That remained home until Daddy returned from the war. But desire for that little student's desk was prophetic.

Which brings up a question that as yet, seems to have no answer. When and how is each person's psychological profile established? All I know for sure is that I am today the same person psychologically as I was in that sandbox. I remember; and my lifelong choice of scholarship and profession, however developed, was locked in before we left Albuquerque. Not developed with intellectual awareness or maturity but established none-the-less before age five.

Al, Sr., Nell and "Little Al" outside Albuquerque Apartment

I am in danger of getting ahead of my story. Bit by bit, you will see how the working out of these "prophesies"–the sandbox experience and the desk, and two more prophesies yet to come in junior high – were to be the main foundations of my identity and work for the first half of my life and even into old age.

II

The Steam Shovel – Some Children Die

"Suffer little children, to come unto me..."
Lk 18: 16

In Texas now-a-days we sometimes hear "This ain't my first rodeo!" Well, I have had a couple of "rodeos" of a type. The first began at the McLemore farmhouse just north of Hazlehurst, Mississippi, when I was almost three. At that age, almost nothing can be remembered, except that I was sitting on the bottom wooden step leading up to the front porch. And I remember the happy old farm dog.

He came up wagging his tail, panting in the late summer heat. I had no defense at that age. He gave me a most liberal tongue bath; hands, arms, eyes, ears, mouth – a total face wash. A couple of days later he was showing symptoms of rabies. I don't remember the series of rabies shots to the stomach I received. The second "rodeo" came three years later at Hazlehurst.

I saw the dog as he entered the gravel driveway that ran between grandma Gommie's house and the house close next door. He saw us, too, and came running up the driveway. It was late April. My cousin Howard, age three and I, age five and a half, were playing under the Mimosa tree outside the kitchen door. I was sitting in my pedal car; stretched out my hand, "Nice doggy!"

To this day, I still see that dog clearly in my mind's eye. Probably part bulldog, but bigger–heavy; running at full tilt. Too late, I understood foaming mouth and an enraged growl.

He hit so hard the pedal car went over on its side. As it righted, he took three or four bites around my right eye, turned and ran away. He was found the next day, dead in a woodlot across the street.

A Day before the Dog Attack

For the rest of their days, Grandma Gommie, my mother Nell, and Aunt Ora May praised the work of Hazlehurst's country practitioner, old Doctor McDonald. He saved my right eye, but there remained the question of rabies.

My five-year-old body had a terrible reaction to the first shot of serum. The serum dose had to be cut in half and in half again (i.e., four times as many shots.) And there were complications beyond that. I had to be hospitalized.

The hospital doctor up in Jackson, Mississippi, showed me his little rubber hammer, demonstrated that it would not hurt and tapped my legs just below the knee to check for reflexes. He nodded once and my parents left. I was wheeled to a polio ward in the same hospital; scared and feeling abandoned; but that was the only place equipped to handle my extensive needs.

This was late April 1946. The Nation was still standing down from the greatest war known to man. The clinic was housed in a hastily built wartime extension to an existing hospital on a low hill just north of downtown Jackson, Mississippi. For three months, a single barracks ward in that polio clinic was my whole world.

There were ten Army-style open ward wooden barracks interconnected to each other and to the original hospital by a long covered wooden hallway. Each ward was entered from the hall through wide double doors. At the other end of each ward, more double doors led down a wooden ramp to the lawn. The exterior was stark white, except for the light grey wooden ramps.

In our ward, there were twenty-four single pipe beds typical of the era, twelve on each side of a wide center aisle. The foot of each bed was at the center aisle. Everything was white in the interior—walls, ceiling, bed linens, hospital gowns, nurses' uniforms and breathing masks; everything except the light grey floors and the shiny brass housings of the iron lungs. Each bed was occupied by a little boy, four to six years old. It was a closed world of fear, suffering, hope and play.

Fear: The nurses had arranged a kind of hierarchy among the beds. The sicker the child, the closer to the hall doors they were assigned for faster access in an emergency. I being the only one without polio was assigned the bed at the extreme far end of the ward, on the right side next to the double doors and ramp to the outside world. I was essentially well, except for an extensive shot program and close monitoring for rabies or acquired polio symptoms. That included four or five shots a day for three months: a quarter dose of rabies vaccine, a "liver shot," whatever that was, and others for unknown purposes.

We all knew what was across the hall. The death ward. And the kids in the iron lungs, next to the hall door, had the most to fear. A gaggle of nurses would suddenly appear at the hall door in the middle of the night, quietly surround the bed of an iron lung resident, connect a portable power pack and wheel him, iron lung, bed and all, out the door and across the hall. As soon as our doors closed, one of the boys still able to walk would hobble to the doors, peek through the crack in the door and announce, "They went across the hall!" They never came back. On one occasion, I saw and made the announcement, myself.

<u>Suffering</u>: Silent suffering within the iron lungs was obvious, but there also was, for little boys not in an iron lung who just wanted to run and play, the difficulty or impossibility of walking at all. All the boys in the middle of the ward and up to my end of the room had some impediment. Some just limped a little; others might drag one or both legs. Closest to the iron lungs were those who could not get out of bed without a wheelchair or nurse carry.

Those of us who could, when there was no nurse in the room, would assist the disabled by picking up dropped toys, bartering and delivering contraband (more on that later), passing notes or drawings—stuff like that. But even those of us fully mobile were breaking rules to place a foot on the floor.

Hope: There always was, this side of those iron lungs, hope for better days, and death was only discussed the morning after someone's trip across the hall. We knew that while some went across the hall, others eventually went home.

Little boys do not get credit due. They are not yet articulate enough to voice their thoughts, feelings and understandings to adults, but there was a kind of common understanding and little boy wisdom that developed up and down the aisle as we saw death and life move through the room.

Play: This is where the contraband came into play. No matter how hospital clean the ward was kept, there always was something to find, capture, trade or swipe. Most coveted were small wheeled toys that could be rolled about the bed *and* paper scraps, rubber bands, string and hair pins.

When rubber bands and paper scraps were in sufficient supply, war would break out; each boy defending his fort, his bed, by firing tight little paper wads at anybody within range. Hairpins, when found, made for long range projectiles to attack far down the line of forts. These were joyous, rollicking occasions allowing even those who could not participate to forget their fear and suffering, at least until a nurse heard the noise. Usually, we could hear them coming down the hall at a fast pace on those noisy wooden floors!

On July 4th that year, I gained some momentary fame. There was a shower of marble sized hail that afternoon. The double doors to the ramp and lawn were left open on that hot July Mississippi day (no A/C). I had hidden away a little toy pickup truck and a long string, so I let that truck roll down the ramp on the string, collected a few falling, bouncing hailstones on each attempt, and shared all that I captured with the other boys. The nurses saw me; just watched and smiled. They, too, must have suffered by association and witness to dying children.

+

A momentary digression. The winter before the dog attack, Grandma Gommie had her gallbladder operation. I was not allowed in the recovery room when the adults went to visit, so I sat out front (I was newly five) watching a steam shovel excavate for a hospital addition.

Steam Shovel

Steam still was king as 1946 began and that shovel was a sight to behold. Huffing and puffing and blowing steam and smoke; the roar of the fire in the boiler firebox; the operator clearly seen, sweating in the boiler-hot open cab, maneuvering the big shovel by levers and valves. He stopped once to shovel more coal into the firebox, then continued to excavate. Fascinating! From that day, my greatest desire was to have a big toy steam shovel. But the war had just ended, and metal was in short supply. Metal toys were hard to find.

+

Back to the polio ward. A few days after the hail, a nurse came to my bed and said, "Come see!" At the open doors, at the bottom of the gray ramp stood my dad in uniform and my mother. He held in his hands the most beautiful thing I had ever seen. A big metal toy steam shovel: with a bright red roof, black smokestack, grey sides; with fully moving parts which he demonstrated for me.

They could not come any closer, but my mother said, "Daddy is here for a short visit. When he comes back, he will stay home, and you can come home, too!"

III

The Loner – Prophecy:
Acts Three and Four

You can hold back from the suffering of the world, you have free permission to do so and it is in accordance with your nature, but perhaps this very holding back is the one suffering that you could have avoided.

Franz Kafka (1883-1924)
Prague born Austrian writer

Daddy did come home at the end of July '46, and so did I. He found employment as a bookkeeper at Iberia Sugar Cooperative, a sugar mill at New Iberia, Louisiana, in the heart of Cajun country. It did not take him but a year or two to become the business manager of the mill. Not bad for a guy who never finished high school! He was mostly self-taught, an avid reader, though he did take a few accounting courses at Tulane University, New Orleans, in his early years.

And joyfully, I entered first grade at Live Oak Elementary, engaging my Albuquerque school desk dream. Not all my classmates shared in my joy. I remember a little girl sitting in the back row who cried uncontrollably for two weeks, even when her mother came and sat next to her.

For me, the trouble started late winter, early in '48: second grade. After all these years, it still is painful to relate. It suppressed the first half of my life and even now has lingering effects. But I must tell it because my life was built upon it.

I am at my natural best, thriving, when people are around – a strong extrovert. Don't even have to know them, they don't have to know I am present. The extrovert gains psychic energy in the presence of a group. But isolate me, and I lose energy rapidly. My chronic isolation began in this way.

South Louisiana warms up quickly after a short, cool winter. Late in February 1948, on the first very warm day, a teacher appeared at the bottom of the front steps at the old three-story brick school (it had an oil fired boiler on the first floor, steam heated classrooms on the second and third). It was the beginning of recess.

"Everybody to the back," she yelled. "Everybody has to play!" I was sitting on the big roots of the ancient Live Oak out front, the tree that gave the school its name. Dutifully, I walked to the back with all the other boys.

We gathered at a place they called a "ball field." Two older boys chose up teams. I was the very last chosen. At age seven, I still was small, emaciated, weak and sickly due to a variety of juvenile illnesses; still in lingering recovery from rabies treatments and the three months of bed confinement. I was sent out to right field.

"Where?" Someone pointed and I went that way, looking around in confusion. The first time a ball came my way, I was not aware 'till it hit the ground nearby. Not knowing what to do, I continued to stand where they told me to go, while everybody was yelling at me, "Pick up the ball; throw the ball." Throw it where? And I was too weak and inept to get it anywhere close to the nearest player. The first time I actually caught a ball, it hurt my hand and dropped to the ground. Finally, someone came out and gave me a glove.

They might as well have strapped a plank to my left hand. It was oversized for my small, weak hand and impossible to flex.

First time at bat they had to show me which end of the bat to hold. As you might imagine, I was a disaster for my team. What was going on? I had never, ever seen a baseball field, a baseball, a glove, a bat or a baseball hat; much less ever having held or used one. Until that day, I did not know these things existed. I had never heard of the game of baseball. TV was not available until the 1950s, I never heard a game on radio, and what was baseball to little boys of the polio ward who could not walk or play?

The same routine was followed the next day. "Everybody must play!" This time, the team captains went through their ritual of choosing teammates. Then, they repeated the ritual just for me. The loser had to take me. I still did not understand what was going on. I was yelled at a lot, adding to my confusion, but nobody thought to take me aside and explain anything. I looked for a teacher to help, but they all were over in the shade of the building, talking in a tight circle of lawn chairs.

I suffered all the shame and contempt and insults and physical shoving and name calling I could stand. On the third day, I hid behind the old oak and when the coast was clear, ran over to the bamboo boundary fence. I hid in its shade until classes resumed. This was repeated many a time, many a day that year. No one ever noticed my absence or came looking for me. Outside of class time, I lived in recess isolation the rest of that school year.

There was no help at home either. My dad refused my appeals that he teach me to throw and catch and swing the bat. Mom would say, "Your dad works hard, He is tired."

+

It was only in my late 40's that I understood what had been going on. As an adult, I was diagnosed with clinical depression and quickly cured. In my dad's day, it could neither be diagnosed nor cured. People would say, "He's just melancholy." He wasn't just melancholy; he was sick! Exhausted by deep clinical depression. And so, I then realized, had been his father.

And that is why my father was incapable of giving me what we now call "quality time." The one time my mother nagged him into playing catch with me in the back yard, he threw the ball three times; said, "That's enough!" Went back inside, leaving me crying in the back yard. That was the first of many times, young as I was, that I thought of suicide, though I never implemented plans to do it.

I will spare you the details of years of isolation brought about by a disastrous introduction to baseball and admit that much of the isolation was self-inflicted. Children and adults often act out what they expect, and I expected that I was unacceptable to others; isolated and alone, I assumed, because I was physically unattractive, inept and unlovable—useless and physically ugly! That assumption lasted into my late twenties. And so, to avoid the pain of expected rejections, I tended to withdraw throughout my school years and early adult life. Withdrawal, of course, only lead to more expectations of rejection and became a self-sustaining reality. The only benefit was that it gave me plenty of time to study, and I excelled in classwork without fail.

But I Thought I Was Ugly!

Around age nine, I expressed a third prophecy. (The first two were mentioned in Chapter I, in the kindergarten. That I would join the USAF and would be a scholarly type.) During a visit to New Orleans, our family attended a symphonic concert. At the intermission, my mother asked me which instrument I would like to play. After a minute of careful consideration, I said, "I want to be the guy with the stick," i.e., the conductor, the boss, the "commander."

The initial baseball experience eventually led to another prophecy as well. In the seventh grade, after years of repeated isolation, often self-inflicted, sometimes due to actual peer rejection, peers still refused to let me play on their baseball team.

At a noon recess, I wandered alone over to a dirt baseball field in the corner by the football stadium. I stood there by myself for the entire noon recess. As the class bell rang, I picked up a stick, wrote big letters in the bare dirt. ALONE. I said out loud, "OK, I'll be a loner. The hell with them. If they won't let me play, someday I will control their ballfield."

And in a metaphoric sense, that is just what I did in adult life.

IV

The Unchosen Life;
A Degree Not Desired

So act as to treat humanity, whether in thine own person or in that of any other, in every case as an end withal, never as a means only.

Immanuel Kant (1724-1804)
German philosopher

"Your father...," my grandma Gommie once said, "...is a good man." So he was. He was faithful to my mother; kept beans on the table, a roof over our head. Returning after World War II, he worked long hours at that sugar mill and was home every night to eat supper, read his newspaper, read a book and go to bed. My dominant memory of him is the back of his newspaper. I write this without rancor. That is just the way it was. He was unchurched, never spoke about religion except once when I was 15. He took me aside and said, "I want you to know; never marry a Catholic and it would be best if you never dated one." That was his sum total of religious comment and instruction for me.

He also, probably, was a strong introvert. He kept his inner life to himself with a vengeance. Rarely would he tell us kids anything about his early life. When in the evening strongly extroverted little Al gathered his books and notes to lay down at the foot of his dad for study, at the first turn of his newspaper I would be noticed and sent to my room "so you can study."

He sent me into isolation night after night where I quickly lost psychic energy, crawled into bed and sometimes cried myself to sleep. He never checked on me, never understood.

But the pressure was constant that I make good grades. So much so that only an "A+" garnered any praise. An "A" brought little comment since that is what he expected of me. An A- was rewarded with a "You can do better!" A "B+" was a cause for alarm and a plain "B" was considered a failure. Never mind that I always was at or near the top of every class, competing well at the state level in biology and physics. I even taught the trigonometry class during my senior year. Neither the "teacher", nor any other high school faculty member had ever been taught that subject. "Teacher" sat in the back, took notes and did the homework I assigned like the rest of the class.

So as graduation approached, Dad asked, "What do you want to study in college?" I was interested in physics, math and teaching, but had not decided. So, he said, "Fine, then you will be an electrical engineer. They make the most money." End of discussion. No discussion at all. That was it. Again, the voice of clinical depression. Subject closed. He could not deal with my uncertainty.

+

There are two things to say about that first semester in college. All 300 engineering students were rounded up in a big auditorium. The speaker had us all look at the person in front, behind, left and right as we sat. Then he said, "Half of you won't be here next semester." He was dead on. The second semester roundup produced very close to 150 remaining engineering students. The killer was math. Which was my best subject. Loved the stuff! Analytical geometry and calculus opened up a whole new world of intellectual knowledge. Wonderful!

The second thing to say about that first undergraduate semester, is that after entrance exams, most of the engineering students were sent to remedial English. I was the only freshman engineer sent to advanced English literature. Which also I loved. So much so, that after the last class, I cried quietly while walking across campus to the dorm; knowing that my dad would not permit a change to an English major. I could hear him say, "You can't make any money with *that!*"

But after years of high school and collegiate isolation and angst, after quietly living through multiple bouts of depression, it turned out that dad had made a good decision for me, for all the wrong reasons.

Late in my junior year, it dawned on me that I had no interest in working as an engineer, it was the math I loved. But I was not going to be a mathematician, either; at the same time, I rejected engineering, I hit the wall. The math wall: it was advanced differential equations. Lucky to make that "C." Hard as I tried, I was not going any further with math. But still, I had to complete my engineering degree.

At the start of the senior year, one elective remained to be chosen. The list of available classes was uninspiring, but there was a course titled "Introduction to Management"; whatever *that* was. I signed up, went to the bookstore and bought the text. Went back to the dorm and opened *Introduction to Management* by Terry.

Amid reading the text introduction, before I started the first chapter, I discovered my real identity: completed my engineering degree, accepted a commission in the United States Air Force and went right to work *managing* the development of classified, special purpose radar systems! Thanks, Dad!

V

The Reminiscence
Ale and Rum *Con Amour*

My love, you will go first to God but not without before having memorized my face. Then one day you will descend by my angel's side to gather up my dust and when he has reformed it in glory be the first to say: Amen!

Ronda Chervin

Late September reminiscence, 2015: I had, for some weeks, been declaring the return of the "class A" bachelor. So speaks the head, but the heart needed more. The head is logic, the heart symbolic. And so, to get the message from the head to the heart, a simple symbolic ceremony was due.

At B & J pizza where we often had supped, seated alone at a small table for two, staring at her empty seat opposite while sipping a bottle of Bass Pale Ale, I pulled the pin on my club sandwich and announced to the bottle, "I have returned." Though the bottle of Ale nodded not, he seemed to understand and accept, blessing my announcement with the next sip of tasty brew. If my return was acceptable to him, then my heart could acknowledge the logical fact. She's gone.

You might be asking yourself, "So what does that bottle have to do with your alleged ceremony? What ceremony?" Your question calls up memories of my last year of previous bachelorhood: late Fall of 1966. I had just turned 26. We were installing a radar near the west end of Bermuda. I was staying at Hamilton AFB bachelor quarters on the east end of the island.

Near sunset one evening, I walked into a bar right on a commercial wharf near the base. A small tramp steamer was tied alongside. At first, golden rays of the setting sun lit up the open face bar like fire, soon blocked by that steamer, plunging the room into cool shade. A couple was seated at the bar counter, early forties, in quiet conversation. We, with the bartender, were the only ones in the room. "Yes, Sah, what will you have, Sah?" (A uniform is a wonderful thing, and I had just made Captain.)

I did not know what I wanted, only not anything not British. After all, this was Bermuda, British territory. I stalled, then noticed the couple were drinking from bottles not seen before. The bright red triangle trademark on the bottles beaconed, so I inquired. It was Bass Pale Ale. The trademark was Britain's first, dated from 1835; the Ale first produced in 1777. Promptly, I joined them in conversation with my own bottle, learning they were off that aforementioned tramp steamer, traveling the world as guests of the skipper. And I thought I had a good deal, traveling to Bermuda at USAF expense!

It was at that bar that I evoked in conversation my firm intent to remain a lifelong bachelor and announced fealty to Bass Pale Ale. No more beer for me! Ale, forever! And certainly, no wife! I had no way of knowing that SHE was just five months away. SHE would change everything!

So, at B & J pizza that evening in 2015, it was proper to announce to that bottle of Bass with renewed commitment, SHE is truly gone, I am back. It took nearly 50 years, but "I have returned." The triangle trademark seemed to give me a welcoming wink as a drop slid down the side of the bottle. Or was that a tear? That was a few weeks after she died.

+

But during '66 and '67, I was living on a sailboat at Diamond 99 Marina, just south of Cape Canaveral. I was in my mid-twenties, the world still was new. I was a bit player on the Apollo moon landing program and living on a sailboat under the Florida sun was my personal paradise. I had announced multiple times to the folks at work that I was to be a lifelong bachelor. I was having too much fun!

That radar we installed at Bermuda was the last of eight identical sets. Prior to the Bermuda caper, we installed a set at Miami

Beach and the Bahama island of Carter Cay, on Grand Turk Island, at Antigua, West Indies, on Ascension Island in the South Atlantic, and at Trinidad, just off the coast of South America.

Carter Cay was something of a management nightmare in that its half-built support building blew down in a storm one night, and later, when the truck mounted radar set was being shipped to Carter on an old WWII Landing Ship, Tank (LST), the bow door of the LST fell off and sank offshore from Palm Beach. Very embarrassing! But the confession I have to make was not about Carter Cay, but Trinidad; more specifically, the Trinidad oxcart.

While I was managing the program, the technical work was being accomplished by a small team of Pan Am and RCA engineers. We all were young, mid-twenties. That should give you a clue as to what is coming.

I accompanied Bob and Mike and one other on their trip to select a site for the radar. It was to be built somewhere high on a certain Trinidad mountain road. They stayed several nights at the Hilton while I bunked in at Chagaramas Navy Base.

When the work was done, still, we had to wait for airlift back to the States. In those days, that meant a long ride on "Old Shaky," a C-124. Old Shaky had the wings and engines of a B-29 attached to a bulbous cargo carrying air frame. Slow as a Piper Cub, but ultra-reliable. What to do with a spare night?

We went downtown in Port of Spain, Trinidad. Ate the wares of street venders (turmeric laced chicken burritos, complete with bones) and got ourselves sloshed on bottles of Trinidad rum while walking around. I was sloshed pretty good but stopped in time. My guys were completely out of control.

We were conscious enough to remember our early morning flight, so we staggered back toward the upside-down Hilton. The upside-down Hilton is built against a sheer cliff with the main entrance and lobby on the top floor; i.e., we had a long uphill walk ahead of us. We started up, soon overtook an old farmer with an oxcart load of hay. No idea why he was out that late, but there he was.

My trio of technical support fumbled around in their pockets (hard to do while staggering and stumbling with a half empty bottle of rum) and came up with what must have been a sizable sum, as gauged by the wide eyes of the old farmer. They clambered aboard and we started up the hill again. The old farmer walked alongside his ox, I followed behind on foot. My team aboard the ox cart was whooping and hollering, waving their near empty bottles in the air and demanding higher speed.

Pedal to the metal, at top speed a good ox can cruise along at a mile and a quarter per hour. Which meant that it took us awhile as the farmer, the ox and I plodded along together. Eventually, we arrived under the Hilton portico to be greeted by an immaculately uniformed doorman, at which point....

My technical trio rolled out the back of the oxcart dragging half the hay load with them. There they lay in a pile of hay at the doorman's feet, laughing and giggling and waving their now empty bottles. The old

Albert E. Hughes

farmer, the ox and I speedily departed at a mile and a quarter per hour, leaving the hay and three quivering corpses to the doorman's disposal. I have no idea how I got back to the base.

We all were young and single. And most folks survive their twenties. Maybe you have been there, too. Now back to more important stuff at Diamond 99 Marina, south of Cape Canaveral.

You may have seen pink elephants once or twice in your young life, and there is the movie "The Pink Submarine," a hilarious spoof on WWII movies; but have you ever seen a 45-foot, cutter rigged *pink* cruising catamaran? I was standing out on the dock at Diamond 99 one evening when such an apparition appeared, turning into our narrow channel. The skipper had a heck of a time turning sharply starboard around a low wall protecting our little marina but made it on the third attempt; tying up in the adjacent dock next to my sailing sloop, "Jabberwocky." Helping with his dock lines, quickly I met the skipper.

Ed Bond, a Boeing engineer from Seattle, designed and built the pink catamaran *Con*

Amour in his back yard. Transferred to New Orleans, later to Cape Canaveral for the Apollo moon landing program, he sailed 'er from Seattle, through the Panama Canal and back to the States.

Departing Seattle

Ed and Marilyn Bond, living aboard with their youngest foster daughter, little Valerie, had three teen foster daughters back in Seattle. And the elder Bonds had a plan. After they got to know me, foster daughter number one showed up. I was polite but disinterested. After a few weeks, she went back to Seattle. Soon, foster daughter number two showed up. Now, I was suspicious, but polite and disinterested. Did not date that one either. In due time she left, to my relief.

But then Marilyn Bond started saying, "Jeannie is coming to visit. You'll *like* Jeannie!" There! No doubt; suspicions confirmed! On the immediate weekend, I arranged for dock space in another town. I was to move the following weekend.

Jeannie arrived on that Tuesday, late in March. Promptly, I was invited to dinner on the *Con Amour*. Apparently, Jeannie knew of the plan, too, because she, setting the table, glared at me when I stepped into their wing deck salon.

Still, with the move scheduled for Saturday, I had not arranged for a weekend date. On Friday after work, I invited Jeannie to go out. We wound up in a nightclub booth, with a small dance floor and a noisy local band. After our first dance, we returned to sip our drinks. I offered a second dance; she said "No."

I said, "Good!" It turned out that neither of us liked to dance. We started talking, a conversation that lasted 48 years.

And of course, she was Catholic, despite my dad's warning never to marry one. Funny thing, though. Ed had told Jeannie never to marry an engineer, a military man or a non-Catholic. I met all three of those specifications!

Courtship

Courtship. *Con Amour*, Ship of Chaperone, following

VI

The Sailing
At Sea with She

For woman...love alone give(s) full stature, as (in) man...spirit alone endow(s) his...highest meaning. Therefore, both seek a psychic relation because love needs the spirit, and the spirit love, for their fulfillment.

Carl Gustav Jung

The subject of pending marriage had been settled before the end of May. By some unremembered decision process, the date was set at 30 September. It probably had something to do, in part, with the plan for that summer. In June, Jeannie and I set out from Diamond 99 aboard the *Con Amour* as crew with Ed, Marilyn and little Valerie, bound for the Caribbean. Limited to six weeks leave, we would reach San Juan, Saint Croix and Saint Thomas, returning via San Salvador, Cat Island and Nassau.

From the beginning, the trip was not uneventful. Already, I knew Marilyn hated living aboard and refused to learn sailing skills. She put us on the sand in the Intracoastal Waterway the first night, down toward Fort Pierce. She was on the helm in the dark around ten pm. Got fixated on a flashing red channel light in the moonless evening. The channel turned left at the light; she didn't.

Lying on my bunk resting before the midnight watch, the sound of sand scraping the bottom of the hull under my bunk was unmistakable. Reaching the cockpit, I saw Marilyn still sitting there, hands on the wheel, staring straight ahead into the darkness of the shore. The red flasher continued to do so about six feet from the starboard hull. She barely missed it.

The next morning, Ed and I went over the side, levered *Con Amour* back into the channel with a long 2" x 6" carried strapped on deck for just such purposes. We proceeded on to Palm Beach inlet. Ed decided Marilyn only would stand the helm during daylight hours and she would cook. He took the evening watch with Marilyn as a carefully watched assistant. Jeannie and I took the midnight watch.

Jeannie, an experienced sailor from her eighteenth year, had been on that initial sail from Seattle to New Orleans.

Departing the Palm Beach inlet, we took our departure due east at the Palm Beach sea buoy aboard the pink catamaran *Con Amour*. The Gulf Stream at an average three knots north would lift us clear of the Bahama bank. Navigation was dead reckoning between noon sun sights, taken with my Plath sextant. We estimated San Juan in seven to ten sailing days.

With two hulls, *Con Amour* had six compartments, three in each hull. In the port hull, fore to aft: a bunk room (Ed preferred to call it a stateroom), the chart room and table, and the aft bunk room. In the starboard hull a forward bunk room, a mid-hull galley and an aft bunkroom. The extreme ends of both hulls and underfloor throughout contained sealed in foam for flotation. *Con Amour* would stay afloat even if awash. The wing deck between the hulls housed a multipurpose living/ dining salon with seating for six.

In the cockpit aft, she had wheel steering to twin rudders, a central mounted diesel out-drive underneath, much like a large outboard motor. The out drive was lifted out of the rushing water that flowed between the hulls when under sail. *Con Amour* was cutter rigged with a main, jib and foresail. Mast height was 45 feet. She could maintain eight or nine knots in a good breeze.

The first two days were a whole sail close reach in three-foot seas with the Bahama bank south of us to moderate wave height. We saw no other traffic except two Soviet ships passing close aboard on their way to Cuba. In those days, Soviet ships were painted a pale green with red scythe and hammer emblems on the stack. The crews on deck seemed cheerful enough, waving as they passed close aboard. Probably delighted to be in warmer waters!

Al at Forestay

Clearing the northern Bahamas, the fetch increased dramatically. Soon we were on a hard beat in six-foot seas. (A beat is well named! Going to windward in heavy seas starts like a fun fight with hard pillows, but becomes unending, pounding tedium in short order.)

It turned out I was the only one who could stay below decks in heavy seas. Everyone else stayed on deck to avoid sea sickness. So often, I wound up cooking what became Al's famous one pot meal. We ate a lot of Dinty Moore stew! Jeannie could stay below deck for a short while, so I cooked and she delivered!

We were doing well to the east, but not enough south. Ed, the skipper, began to fret and about the fourth day while resting in my bunk, suddenly I heard the diesel fire up. Ed had decided to help nature a bit. This he continued to do as needed to get the required southing. Meanwhile: pound, pound, pound into increasing seas with constant spray and a couple of inches of water running across the deck. On several occasions, sail tending at the forestay, I was thrown up in the air a few feet. Great Adventure! Jeannie had little experience sail trimming, but well had learned the skill of steering in rough seas and always was ready to take her turn if the men tired.

We barely were able to get south enough to see Grand Turk's north point light at dusk, lying right on the horizon. (Several times I had been on that island, as one of the USAF test range bases was on the south end.) Finally, in the lee of Hispaniola the next night, the wind and seas moderated. We were back to gentle breezes and two-foot seas or less. As the night progressed, the winds dropped to nil and the diesel kept us moving. Jeannie and I took the midnight watch.

Blue water sailing at night has its own effects and mysteries. Especially on calm, moonless, pitch black nights; the sea seems on fire with green light around the hull. The passing of the hull and breaking wavelets excite millions of plankton to turn on their lights. The boat's wake leaves an eighth of a mile of fire behind.

During long night hours on the helm you likely will start hearing voices. All blue water sailors know these voices. Indistinct voices that seem to appeal for rescue. You must ignore those voices, a product of your own mind. Long distance solo sailors have been lost when they went overboard in search of persons not there in the darkness. At the wheel after midnight, steering by a star at the horizon, Jeannie and I talking quietly, she drowsing at my side from time to time, I heard those voices that night north of Hispaniola.

Finally, at sunrise on the tenth day, we were motoring north of Puerto Rico, about

50 miles offshore in a dead calm. We noticed behind us a large power cruiser coming up fast. He roared up to us, cut power, drifted alongside, a little longer than our 45 feet and the skipper leaned out from the upper cockpit. He yelled, "WHICH WAY TO PUERTO RICO?!" We pointed. With a salute, he roared off to the south. We, too, soon turned to motor south in dead calm toward San Juan.

Al at the Wheel Under Power, Calm Seas.
Ed Bond at left.

Right in the harbor entrance late afternoon, Ed ran out of fuel. There we sat utterly becalmed in the wind shadow of Morro Castle. Which was bad enough, but around 6pm a Navy squadron of four destroyers and a surfaced attack submarine, out playing hide and seek all day, pulled up behind us a quarter mile and shut down. We had the harbor blocked! After another hour or so, the Coast Guard sent out a small boat and towed us into the harbor most in-gloriously to the nearest fuel dock alongside the airport runway. The Navy squadron commander was not pleased! He burned Ed's ears on the radio.

We rested a day and two nights at San Juan, then sailed east. Ed still was depending on the diesel in light airs to move us along on our limited schedule, but he was determined not to run out of fuel again. He topped off at Saint Croix.

While he was refueling, Jeannie and I took a short walk along the beach road, quietly talking, hand in hand. It was somewhere during that walk I first realized this was not just a proposed marriage, but truly we already were inseparable as one. I had assumed the masculine role of protection and care without any conscious effort. She was my sounding board, becoming my spiritual guide though it would be years before I would fully understand that. This wasn't going to change; I did not want it to change.

Fueled up, we continued east, bound for Antigua, West Indies. Around noon on the third day Jeannie was at the helm, I was sitting next to her on the port bench watching the water pass by. We were a couple of hundred miles from any land when suddenly I realized, "Ed! I can see the bottom! I see starfish and seaweeds on the bottom!"

I heard Ed at the chart table say, "Good! Now I know exactly where we are." And indeed, if you check the sea charts, there is a sea mount out there, only 25 feet below mean sea level. Deadly to ships and of breaking wave danger to yachts in heavy weather but calm that day. We sailed right over it! A few minutes later, Ed came on deck and announced "We are out of time. Can't make Antigua and return to Florida on time."

A light southeasterly trade wind had come up. We would be turning with wind on the stern (jibing). The risk is that the boom could sweep across the deck hard and fast. A careless jibe can tear the rigging right off the boat or knock a crewman overboard and unconscious. I took the wheel for the jibe.

Jeannie close hauled the boom. With the boom in tight a-board, loudly I announced, "Jibe-Oh!" Turning, the mains'l boom crossed the cockpit under control and we set sail on a port side broad reach north by northwest to a comfortable sail for Saint Thomas, sans diesel noise and smell. Fair winds and following seas! We sailed into Charlotte Amalie harbor on Saint Thomas the second day, following.

Safely at dock, we wandered down to the end to check out a strange sight. It was young John Rushing's *Sea Egg*, 9' 6" long, painted gray and true to its name shaped like an egg with a mast and rudder. John soon was located and invited to dinner aboard the *Con Amour*. He was newly arrived from Plymouth, England and was attempting a circumnavigation record in the smallest boat ever. He regaled us with tales of a shoving match with a mama whale who mistook the *Sea Egg* for one of her young. He wanted to go west; mama wanted him to join her on a more southerly tack.

And there was the time he was becalmed, dropped his hat in the water. He reached down to pick it up and found his hand to be on the back of a shark that was somewhat larger than *Sea Egg*. He quickly decided the shark needed the hat more than he.

(A month after we returned to Florida a tiny news article in *Yachting Magazine* reported that John had cleared the Panama Canal bound for Hawaii and never was seen again.) All blue water sailors know the risks.

After a couple of days, we pressed on to the west, arriving offshore from San Juan after dark, another moonless night. We had to find the green, three-second flasher buoy marking the harbor entrance. Hard to do on a pitch-black night with blinding city lights in the background. Ed was at the helm, Jeannie and Marilyn sleeping below deck, I was at the forestay. Ed found the light and I, squinting through all the background lights, confirmed: three-second flash, green low on the water. We turned to port and made a run for the harbor. Things were going swimmingly well until I spotted surf in the faint gloom. "BEACH DEAD AHEAD!" I yelled. Indeed, we were no more than 40 yards off the beach, likely closer.

We did a snap U turn (not nautical terminology, I admit) and returned to deep water. Looking back, that light still was there, three seconds flashing green. But now I also could discern that it was amongst some buildings. Jose's Bar and Grill? We will never know. But we did find the harbor marker, just a quarter mile west.

We hung around San Juan a bit too long. Now we had to hustle, and Ed was determined to stop at San Salvador, where Columbus first landed. The trip was uneventful; we arrived at the southeast shore of San Sal, waded ashore, set the hook on the beach. Sure enough, there is a bronze plaque there making the historic claim. If the claim is accurate no sailor, Christopher included, would hang around very long. That beach is to windward. Easily, the easterly trade winds could drive a sailing ship ashore. I have my doubts about that beach as his landing.

After a few minutes, we waded back aboard, sailed around and anchored in the lee of the island. Ed went ashore to the little village, quickly came back. Locals warned him of the horde of mosquitoes that would rise out of the swamp behind the village at sunset. We could have anchored further out, but since we were in a hurry, we decided to leave before dark.

Once clear of the island we found a strong wind building with eight-foot seas on the stern. At the wheel, I could feel the stern lifting. *Con Amour* was no surfboard, but she began to surf down the wave fronts anyway. Twelve knots easy! Lots of fun and dangerous as all get out! I had her pointed downhill for a couple of hours 'till it got too dark to see the next wave ahead of us.

Never go so fast as to stick the bow in the wave ahead. You, too, quickly can be dead. The waves are moving, but the water is not. When the bow hits and stops, the stern keeps going. It is called a pitch pole. Sailboats perform poorly upside down in the air! Taking a more oblique route down the wave fronts, I began to slow the boat and soon the evening breeze began to moderate as well. We continued west with short stops at Cat Island and Nassau, then crossed the Gulf Stream.

Arriving a mile and a half off the Florida shore just after sundown, it became evident in short order that we were near St Augustine, not at Cape Canaveral harbor. The Gulf Stream had pushed us north of our estimates. Tired as all get out and in the dark, we opted for the nearest safe inlet, St John's River at Jacksonville, tying to an unoccupied commercial dock around 2am. After two hours of R&R, we headed back toward the sea.

Short of the sea buoy and in the dark well before dawn, a tug crossed port to starboard ahead of us. We gave him what we thought was plenty of room and continued, planning to turn south at the sea buoy. We passed behind the tug by maybe 200 feet.

I was on the bow, Ed at the helm. Watching the tug, I then turned my attention ahead. "CABLE DEAD AHEAD!" I yelled. Ed started his snap U turn reminiscent of the beach encounter at San Juan. I looked to the left and saw a dimly lit kerosene lantern sitting above me on the bow of a high riding empty barge. Towed by that tug on a long cable, that rusty, almost invisible barge missed us by just a few feet. Easily, it would have rolled us under that high riding bow and the tug crew would not even have noticed! Later, I read that tugs at sea often will tow with as much as a thousand feet of cable to protect the tug from a surging barge.

The Caribbean voyage of the pink catamaran *Con Amour* ended without further incident; she entered Port Canaveral and sailed down the Indian River to Diamond 99.

We all agreed that the proposed marriage would last. As Jeannie put it in her life testimony, forty odd years later, "We battled bad weather, bad tempers, bad smells, tight quarters and all of us battled sea sickness except Al. There was no hiding of bad habits. It was a concentrated courtship in the presence of my foster parents and high seas."

Indeed, we were inseparable for 48 years. During those 48 years, on active duty and in civilian life we lived mutually devoted lives while raising two daughters, Shannon and

Catherine; we lived at Patrick AFB in Florida three separate times and in eleven other states, from Florida to Alaska, from Massachusetts to California, plus the British State of Antigua and Barbuda in the Caribbean. We traveled from Fairbanks, Alaska to Ascension Island in the South Atlantic and to eastern Canada.

For better or for worse, in sickness and in health, until death did we part. I protected her in her multiple illnesses and life-threatening operations; she brought me to God most high and stood by me when I almost died. For both of us it is safe to say that our love for one another extended to unconditional love. She in particular, through our marriage and her inherent goodness, can be called Holy. Upon her death, I published her life testimony, titled *Saint Jeannie's Shiny Black Shoes.*

+

Three years after the sail to the Caribbean and back, from Boston snows we reached Antigua by air, too late for a connecting flight to St Lucia where *Con Amour* was waiting. At a hotel that afternoon, I was flat on my back at the pool wearing nothing but a bathing suit. Jeannie was in the room. Eyes closed, I heard a slight shuffle of feet. Opening one eye, I gazed upon the cheapest bikini I had ever seen, hovering over me. It had to be cheap, because there was almost no cloth to admire. In haste, I opened the other eye to behold the marvelous sight. She might have been 21 and I was barely 29, recently married. The gloriously female vision spoke. "You're in the Air Force, aren't you?"

Cautious of my marital status I responded, "How do you so conclude? I, too, am almost naked."

Pointing under the recliner and my less than glorious male frame, she said, "My daddy makes those shoes for the Air Force." I quickly recalculated to sixteen-jailbait! We separated with a mutual laugh. Sorry, I digressed.

Arriving in St Lucia the next day, two days following, we sailed the pink catamaran *Con Amour* up the west coast of St. Lucia, pausing at a beach near the north point. Skipper Ed Bond gently bumped the sand in three-and-a-half feet of clear water; we set the hook on the beach. The early afternoon glare off the sand was intense, but the tree line was near—actually the dead palmetto line. There was only a scattering of palms. Thirty yards inland on flat terrain, I was walking on several inches of dead palmetto leaf trash over sand. It was awful hot, and the sand seemed unyielding, rock hard. Scratching away the trash and sand with the edge of a sandal, I discovered I was standing on concrete. Looking up, in a straight line for a mile or more to the east and for the width of a runway, there were no trees at all. Later, we found I was standing on a WWII runway, from which B-17s, B-29s and sub hunters had protected our southern flanks.

Mid-afternoon, we set sail for Martinique. On clearing St Lucia's north point, the north-east winter trades came on full force. Forty-five-foot-long *Con Amour* settled down to an estimated eight knots. (At sea on *Con Amour*, we navigated by dead reckoning between noon sun shots. GPS was not yet available. Speed was estimated in the old way, by timing a wood chip floated stem to stern. Worked like a charm!)

Darkness was surreal that night with a deep cloud deck. We were sailing in a black void with no horizon, orientation limited to phosphorescence around the hull. Over time, the psychological effect was foreboding.

Marilyn and Jeannie turned in. I stayed on the wheel all night, sailing solely by compass while skipper Ed went below repeatedly to fuss over and recheck the charts. Finally, he came on deck and said, "Heave to. We should be seeing Martinique's lights reflecting off the clouds."

"Heave to" is sailor talk for stop! To go dead in the water and just sit there. It is accomplished by backing the jib and slacking the mains'l. And so I did.

But there was nothing there. Nothing! Just a black void all 'round us. We sat there in pitch blackness and silence for three hours, seeing nothing but the compass light and an occasional splash of phosphorescence; hearing nothing, second guessing our speed calculations, wondering about our drift compensation in the east to west current that flowed between islands. Course had been offset east to compensate for wind and current drift. All by estimates. But where was Martinique? Where were we?

At the first hint of dawn, just less black, dead to the east, blacker than black a quarter mile away was tall, massive ship rock. Considering the sea drift, in pitch blackness we must have hove to right next to that rock. In another fifteen minutes we could see Martinique's south shore, right in front of us! Another few minutes of sailing would have put us on the rocks below high cliffs.

At port, we learned of the island wide power outage that night.

VII

The Fear – A Fall and Rising

Nothing is so much to be feared as fear.
The man who is dissatisfied with himself,
what can he not do? – Thoreau

The National Cheyenne Mountain Complex (NCMC) is behind massive vault blast doors in a hardened, deep granite cave under Cheyenne Mountain near Colorado Springs CO. The Space Defense Center there occupied two operations rooms separated by a glass upper wall, with open passageways between the rooms at both ends of that wall. In one room, analysts maintained the satellite catalogue.

Albert E. Hughes

Cheyenne Mountain

Differential equations describing each satellite orbit change as satellites are perturbed slightly by gravitational anomalies or in low orbit by occasional impacts of air molecules. Spring of 1973, there were near 7000 objects in the catalogue: actual satellites and orbiting space junk; including an astronaut glove, an errant wrench and a multitude of parts from a Soviet rocket body that blew up on orbit. There was plenty of work for the half dozen analysts, all whizz-kid lieutenants. As a senior Captain, I cross trained to the analyst position to clock operational credentials. It was a welcome change after ten years of radar program management.

The purpose of the catalogue was to know what was up there and exactly where it was at all times, so that we could recognize anything new the Soviets added, like reconnaissance satellites and, heaven forbid, on-orbit weapons. At the time, the Soviets already had launched an experimental FOBS (fractional orbit bombardment system). Fortunately, they later abandoned the concept. If successful, they could have launched a surprise attack from the south while all our detection assets looked north. Also, the analysts calculated and reported probable earth impact points of the larger falling satellites and space junk, anything that could burn through the atmosphere and cause loss of property or life.

The other room housed the Senior Director of the Space Defense Center (a Major) and an enlisted crew, a tech sergeant and several staff members. Their job was to determine and report status on the world-wide radar network that tracked satellites and post essential information for the Director's immediate use. He directed the enlisted crew and the orbit analysts in the next room. The Senior Director's most challenging effort was to determine within two minutes of a Soviet launch what it was, which orbit it was headed for, transmit initial orbital elements and order track by world-wide radars in position to do so. The red phone at his console had Flash and Flash Override capabilities. In a catastrophic emergency, he could knock everyone off the line except the Chairman of the Joint Chiefs and the President.

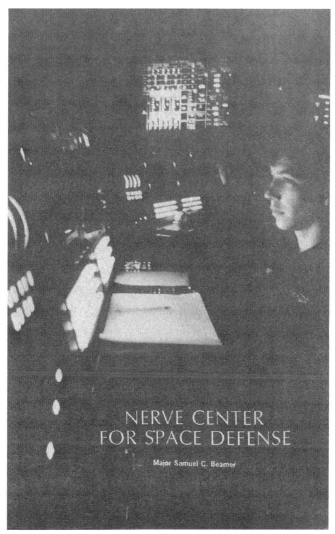

NERVE CENTER
FOR SPACE DEFENSE

Major Samuel C. Beamer

Space Defense Center

The Center's Philco 2000 computer was obsolescent even in my day. It filled several rooms with tape drives elsewhere in the deep underground Complex. With a single card reader in the analyst room, we fed the whole tape-driven contraption.

The Senior Director at the Console

One midnight shift when all the staff sergeants were busy, the tech offered to make the coffee. The pot was kept in a corner of the analyst area beyond the card reader. As he entered the area, he tripped. Thirty cups of scalding hot coffee and a large scoopful of coffee grounds went right into the reader, which promptly choked and stopped working. That shut down the whole effort to keep the catalogue accurate and current.

Easy enough to clean up the floor, but now what? We cleaned up as best we could, but still no go. Accidently, I kicked the bottom right corner at the front of the cabinet. Voila! The card reader came to life. For a couple of minutes, then jammed.

Every time it stopped, that kick dislodged a few more coffee grounds. When I transferred out of the Mountain a few months later, that kick still was operational!

I had cross trained as a satellite orbit analyst. On arrival, I had clear seniority, the only Captain in the room. So, I ran the analyst section for a few months; that job was a joy. After years of math studies and a long wait, finally I was using differential equations most routinely and on a daily basis.

Then my name popped up on the promotion list to Major. I was asked, and gladly accepted the offer to train again, this time as a Senior Director. I went immediately from most senior of all the analysts on all the crews, to the most junior of all the directors on all the crews. But that was not my problem.

The problem was that still, at age 33, I was terrified of public speaking, and on swing shift I would have to brief 30 or so "tourists," mostly military dependents, on tour in the Mountain. I was fine one on one or in small working groups, both as leader and follower. I had no problem as a Major-select waking up the Chairman of the Joint Chiefs of Staff at three in the morning, Washington time, to make a protocol required report. A large deorbiting Soviet rocket body was calculated to hit somewhere in Argentina. We had a pleasant chat while I filled him in on the technical details – almost a calm father and son conversation. (As it turned out, the rocket body entered the atmosphere flat, skipped like a flat rock on a pond, and stayed up another day and a half, finally landing in the Indian Ocean.)

But I was almost neurotic when it came to an audience of strangers. It was so bad that at another time, after briefing my AGM-86 cruise missile test program proposal to the Army's White Sands Proving Ground staff, (remember, I was Air Force) I excused myself, went out into the hall and collapsed! That fear had been with me ever since high school.

(The Army accepted the proposal with enthusiasm and that is where the first tests were run – despite some very unhappy senior Air Force Colonels and a couple of generals, who hated paying the Army for services rendered. Still, White Sands, the most heavily instrumented piece of sand in the Nation at that time, was the right place to be.)

The other problem was Colonel Throckmorton. Nearly all the Senior Directors were afraid of him! I will explain how both fears were overcome.

My trainer was an excellent instructor, a major and Lt Colonel select, who was about to move up and out. I would replace him as Senior Director on Bravo crew. Finally, I confided my fear to him. Regarding the swing shift briefing to public visitors, he said, "Look, Al. First of all, you have the briefing slides. They say it all. Talk to the slides. Second of all, those folks know nothing from nothing. You will be the expert in the room. They will believe anything you say. So, get in there and say it!"

That same evening, he told me about Throckmorton, an Army Colonel. He was a fish out of water, a Command Director in a joint service operation dominated by Air Force officers. He determined which subordinates he could trust by raising hell with them like a drill sergeant and watching the response. My instructor told me all the other Senior Directors were afraid of him, but if I stood up to him when the challenge came, he would trust me. With that advice, he turned all Bravo crew over to me and departed. I never saw him again.

Those simple ideas transformed me. Halfway through the swing shift briefing, it occurred to me that I was actually having fun, switching from stilted talking-to-the-slides to a conversational mode with interested individuals in the tour group. We spent so much time just chatting about the briefing and having a good time that we went overtime; their guide had to step in to move them along.

A week later on the same shift, the attack came. Throckmorton was all over me about something I had done. I stood tall, clarified my actions, gave my rationale and suggested that what I had done was not only justified, but necessary. He paused, thought a moment; said, "OK." Returned to his post.

+

We bought our first house there in Colorado Springs. We knew that a year or so later, I would be sent to a one-year remote assignment, then return to the mountain. The idea was that Jeannie —who was pregnant – would stay in that house during my absence. It did not work out that way, as you will see, but that was the initial plan.

Shannon, our first, was late. Two weeks late. So, we took a ride out in the country on rough backroads; returned just before dark. Right at bedtime, Jeannie already was in bed. I heard her say, "Uh Oh! Guess what broke?!" Didn't get much sleep that night. Shannon was born soon thereafter in The Springs.

It was a whipsaw year for me. Along with conquering my principle fear, speaking in public, it was a first year of home ownership; of death, my Father; of new life, Shannon; of coping with a new idea, fatherhood; anticipating with some angst our pending one-year separation; and for the first time in my life, I was caused to focus, to comprehend and appreciate, the humble, loving charity of a total stranger.

Later the week that Shannon was born, I just had arrived home early morning from a midnight shift at the mountain when the doorbell rang. At the door was a woman with a big cardboard box she hardly could carry. Handing it to me, she said, "You may return these when the baby outgrows them." She turned and walked away without another word.

Jeannie said, "She lives across the street. We talked once a couple of weeks ago." We never did get to know our neighbors. I was on rotating shifts, constantly changing my hours, and Jeannie was housebound learning to be a new mother. The box? All the infant clothing Shannon would need for her first year.

+

As it turned out, I volunteered for remote duty at Clear, Alaska, a ballistic missile early warning radar site (BMEWS). Regulations required that the family must be at least 60 miles from the place of assignment for me to receive remote credit. Fairbanks was 80 miles northeast of Clear with direct rail and highway access.

The following June we sold the house, stored the furniture and drove north through British Columbia and the Yukon to begin our Alaskan adventure! Oh, and Colonel Throckmorton! Did I pass his test?

A couple of months after he challenged me, he retired on a Monday. That last Sunday of his long, distinguished Army career, he and his family had a private, intimate little early spring picnic in a Colorado Springs park. He invited one other couple to join with his family in a bitter-sweet rite of passage. Jeannie brought the salad, and I carried the crib with our infant baby Shannon.

VIII

The Ice Fog – A Cloud of Unknowing

Faith is in its essence simply a matter of will, not reason, and to believe is to wish to believe, and to believe in God is, before all and above all, to wish that there may be a God. And perhaps the sin against the Holy Spirit is none other than that of not desiring God, not longing to be made immortal.

Miguel De Unamuno (1864-1936)
Spanish writer, Rector, U. of Salamanca

Alaskan black bears are not particularly fond of humans, but they are very fond of our food. Scraps from us are treasures to them. So, it was wise to check carefully before approaching one of the dumpsters behind the Clear Station kitchen or club. It was not uncommon to see a fuzzy black head pop up from inside an open dumpster, checking for humans. And on several occasions when an outer kitchen door was left open, the cook found a black bear checking the day's menu in the refrigerators. Or in summer, if the several buildings' interconnecting hallway side doors were open for ventilation, midway between buildings you might find a black bear taking a campus short cut across the hall. They were amiable enough so long as you did not get between mama and her cub or any black bear and his food.

Brown bears are less amiable and very gun shy around humans. They stay well away back in the woods. On the other hand....

While the black and brown bear are named for the color they have, the Grizzly Bear is named for what he does not have. A Grizzly has no sense of humor. None whatsoever. And his more formal name is *Ursus Horribilis,* if you get my drift. The word "grouchy" does not begin to approach their reality. So, shortly after nightfall, I got a Grizzly (a grisly?) phone call on an early fall swing shift, 1973.

The game wardens at Mt McKinley just south of us were rushing the major remaining parts of one of their own to our station. Would we request a med-evac? Which promptly I accomplished from my tactical command console at the radar site.

A warden accidently had walked up on a Grizzly in the last twilight of the day. What did he see? Probably something like you could have seen at the University in Fairbanks.

The University museum was entered through a high ceiling hall. The hall extended away from the main building as does a typical Alaskan mud or snow room. The entrance door was not straight out the end, but out the side at the outer end of the hall. One enters and turns right toward the museum displays, head down; stomping snow off his boots. He is not prepared for what happens.

Instantly, the mind wants to know, "Whose furry brown knees are those?" The head snaps back to find an incredible rack of teeth installed in a huge, furry brown head, about eight feet above the floor, bookended by two enormous claw infested paws, they easily nine feet up. The Grizzly is standing on his hind legs in the attack position. That is a good approximation of what the warden must have seen; but not for long.

He climbed a scrub tree, typical of the area. For the bear, no problem. He knocked the tree down, liberated one of the warden's arms and did a great deal of other incidental damage.

Well within the hour, a medevac plane landed on our uncontrolled gravel strip, picked the pending corpse up and took off for Eielson AFB near Fairbanks post haste. Nevertheless, the warden died on the plane, halfway to Eielson. Sometimes, death is the preferred option.

All that, of course, was on my mind two weeks later, walking alone a half mile up the gravel road to the railroad crossing. There were continuous thickets of scrub trees on both sides all the way along. What was back in there, unseen?

After Labor Day, all the tourists left central Alaska. So, the Alaskan Railway parked their neat, shiny passenger cars; leaving in operation a single rusty, dusty antique passenger car. It was heated by a pot belly, coal fired chimney stove sitting on the floor at the center of the car. They attached that car to the back end of a scheduled freight, the single passenger car followed only by the caboose.

The crossing was at the middle of a four-mile section of straight track. So, when the engine cleared the last curve down south, departing the coal mines at Healy, the first faint glimmer of a headlight could be seen. At the near approach, I gave the perfunctory wave, answered by an acknowledging toot from the old F-2 diesel's horn. But clearly, he was not slowing to stop.

(It *was* an F-2(!), rare even in the early 70's. On a couple of occasions, I was able to talk my way into the cab. The engineers told me they were F-2's; obsolescent hand-me-downs from railroads in the lower 48.)

He rumbled on by at full tilt as I began, out of habit, to count the freight cars. At forty something, here comes the antique passenger car and caboose. The conductor was standing on the back step of the caboose. Hanging on to the step hand hold, he leaned out and in passing yelled over the rumbling freight, "WE'LL BE BAAAAK!" Today? Next spring?

I stood on the track watching that caboose get smaller and smaller down that long straight. Finally, when it reached pin head size, the caboose stopped shrinking. Then it started to grow. They were backing down. After a good ten minutes in agonizingly slow reverse, the caboose reached the present crossing, inching along, and ground to a halt. The conductor stepped down and said, "No brakes."

I entered the caboose, stepped across the coupler into the antique, and sat—not too close to that stove. There was an open coal bin against the side wall and a grizzled old Alaskan in a parka sleeping against the front wall. The conductor collected my fare and returned to his office – the caboose. Next stop, Fairbanks!

We worked six shifts in five days at Clear AFS, then were off for two and a half days. I had a small private bedroom and bath. At

Fairbanks, Jeannie and Shannon lived in a small apartment complex. I stayed with them two days out of each seven. Most of the tenants were military dependents, so it was always party time somewhere in the complex. Shannon had her first birthday party there. When the iced cake was placed before her, she promptly took a cake bath: both hands, head, hair and face.

At another party, we all were sitting on the floor of our small apartment when someone said, "Look at Shannon!" She was standing up for the first time with a big grin on her face. And she was drunk. She had been crawling around on the floor finishing off our guests half empty glasses!

Beside the bears, train travel and family time, another of the delights of that Alaskan assignment was Bravo crew: eight enlisted troops and two younger officers (Captains) to keep track of.

At the start of winter, one Airman, a black man of good size, left on a month's leave. The very next week on the first midnight shift, I sat down at my console—and there he was, sitting at his! Back home in Syracuse, he was attacked by another who broke a pool stick, creating a sharp wooden weapon. My Airman relieved him of it and with the blunt end of the stick, beat him senseless.

Everyone in the pool hall testified that my guy had been attacked, so the police gave him a nice Monopoly Game style choice. Go to jail. Go directly to jail. Do not pass go, do not collect $200; *or* go directly to Alaska. He thought frigid, long-nights-Alaska was looking pretty good about then.

Radar Site, Clear Alaska

My number one, Captain Nick Alexandrov, was just plain fun to have around. The first midnight shift after he joined Bravo crew, he created a minor ruckus down at NORAD (North American Aerospace Defense), deep under Cheyenne Mountain near Colorado Springs. It was four in the morning, Alaskan time.

We were in Alaska to detect Russian missile and spacecraft launches. They were not busy that night, so we had little to do. Try staying awake for eight hours all night doing absolutely nothing. Go ahead! Try it!

Anyway, Nick, sitting quietly at his console to my immediate left suddenly said, "Grandma must be awake now." (Grandma, he explained upon my query, was in New York.) He picks up the phone at his console, punches in the administrative line and connects with the NORAD operator at Cheyenne Mountain. She in turn patches him into grandma's house. He says, "Hi, grandma."

Only Nick said it in fluent Russian. I should have anticipated this. Look at his last name! They continue talking for about twenty minutes in fluent Russian, but in just moments, the tactical operations line lights up on my console.

The operator heard the Russian, informed the Command Director on duty at NORAD and he wanted to know how the hell did the Russians tap into our com network?! For months thereafter, they knew Bravo crew was talking to grandma, every time they heard Russian. Like I say, Nick was fun to have around.

He also had his own bear story. He was out back of the administrative office on a warm spring day, washing his Fiat 124. Nice little sports car. And he was well away from the dumpsters, up in front of the car with a bucket of soapy water. The rinse bucket was on the ground between the Fiat driver's door and the car in the next parking slot. A-rubbin' and a-scrubbin' as he backed around the front left fender, working aft, he hears a puppy dog style "lap, lap, lap, lap...." Unaware, he had backed within touching distance of a black bear cub, helping itself head down to a cool drink.

He turned, saw the bear a bucket width away and sucked in a loud, "Uuaahh! *Simili modo*, the cub looked up and did the same,

"Uuaahh!" They took off running in opposite directions. Fortunately, mama bear was preoccupied in a dumpster some distance away. She was clueless. Wonder what her cub told her that evening?!

Number two Captain was a real concern. He liked beer. Too much he liked beer. There was a time at a roadside bar he got busy slurring and cursing the barkeep and all Alaskans for not having his preferred German brew. The barkeep and a couple of grizzled old prospectors at the bar were not amused. As the prospectors started to get up, I raised my left palm toward them and said, "We've got this one." Nick and I spun number two Captain around on his stool, slid him up on his wobbly feet and marched him arm in arm to the car. Close one! We three were techno-nerds, not bar room fighters.

And the time in the club bar: awaiting the start of the swing shift he noticed through the windows three adult black bears going through the dumpster. Announcing that we should not worry, he would ssccchoo them away, he headed for the back door. Several of us got there first, dragging him back to the table. He needed to be watched all the time.

During the long winter, I had another problem to deal with: me. Deep depression set in. Not clinical; there is a difference. This was just a deep blue funk.

At that latitude, we got little more than an hour of dim winter twilight each day, assuming it was not heavily overcast. The sun would take a ten-minute peek between two mountain peaks south of the station. That was it until the same time next day. The nightly low was minus 45F, sometimes minus 55.

A mild winter, locals said. I also read somewhere, or a local told me, that at minus 55, old fashioned natural rubber tires would shatter like glass. Going outside without arctic gear was a ten-minute trip to the grim reaper. We were told we would have frozen parts before we could get all that gear on. Even in a heated truck we wore arctic gear, just in case of a breakdown: mukluks; fur lined over trousers, fur lined hooded parka with a flap that covered all but the eyes, and fur lined gloves over regular gloves.

In central Alaska, the suicide rate spikes in January and February. And every year at spring thaw in Fairbanks next to a certain bar, they removed a few bodies from the ice breakup in the Chena River – drunks who wandered outside during the winter. At another bar downtown, they were averaging one murder each weekend, year 'round, as prospectors and Indians fought it out. One murder per week in a town of only 14,000. But if you stayed out of that bar, you were perfectly safe.

Most wearing on the psyche was the work routine: rotating shifts every two days with a quick turn between the second mid and the first swing shift. Six shifts in five days followed by a two-and-a-half-day break. Impossible to maintain a normal sleep schedule during the entire one-year assignment. And repeating, weeklong separation from family: my wife and newborn first child at Fairbanks.

One more issue to top it off. Unchurched from the beginning, I was a lifelong agnostic. That worried me: I hoped there was a God but needed and recognized no evidence. Those long, family-separated nights on duty gave me a whole lot of depressing worry time. Finally, at the end of a swing shift late in January, at my bed, I gave it an "Is anybody up there?" type of prayer. Had never thought to ask, before. If somebody was "up there," I just wanted the truth. Just the truth.

I slept well that night for the first time in weeks. I had done all that I could do, I thought. So not to worry. I would not recognize the imparting of grace for several more years.

All in all, it was a great year. I yearn to return. Central Alaska is wild away from Fairbanks and the highway, always beautiful: eternally snow-capped mountains; rivers, lakes and wild-life everywhere; exploding sheets of yellow light sweeping across the night sky, curtains of green light that seem to move in a gentle, unfelt breeze. Shimmering ionosphere at night; daytime glitter of ice fog encrusted trees winking golden light refracted from a horizon-low sun. And sand-dry snow, but most of all, ice fog. Ice fog coated everything in a soft white swede.

All winter in Fairbank's frozen fog and darkness, ghostly apparitions slowly would fade into view from pitch darkness, pass under hovering, fog shrouded streetlights and fade slowly away into darkness: children in their arctic gear walking to and from school. They would do that down to minus 40F. Below that, the schools would close. I yearn to return.

Wait! Wait! Was that a metaphor? You bet it was. Real *and* a metaphor. Vague, dismembered, unsupported, floating images of light and children or cars or anything else that moved in and out of dimly translucent perception. Like my mental state: a fog of unknowing shrouding a night combat of shadows, flashing lights in a black void, distracting thoughts and meaningless noise; all opposing my desire for God against a complete lack of evidence for His being there at all.

IX

The Fire – Transcendent Dawn

In the tender compassion of our God the dawn from on high shall break upon us, to shine on those who dwell in darkness and the shadow of death, and to guide our feet into the way of peace.

Luke 1:69

After the Alaska tour, we drove back down through the Yukon, British Columbia, and on to the east and south to Dayton, Ohio; to Wright-Patterson AFB where I had started my career. There, little Shannon mastered the big wheel slide on our gently sloping driveway and Jeannie delivered Catherine at the base hospital.

I, too, was successful. The Air Force Institute of Technology conferred upon me a Master of Science in Systems Management with distinction, loaded with math electives—enough to have declared a minor in Operations Research—mathematical optimization of system process sequences. Which I did not declare. Had I done so, the USAF may have snatched me up to go in a direction I did not want to pursue.

Toward the end, my classmates expressed considerable worry about me. They all had searched out career enhancing Pentagon jobs while I appeared inactive. I had visited the Pentagon basement with its leaky overhead pipes that dripped water and perhaps sewage onto Majors' desks. If they wanted to start there and work their way upstairs and toward the coveted inner circle, that was fine with me. But after Alaska, I had visions of palms nodding to trade winds and steel drums playing into moonlight hours. I had a better idea and a ticket up my sleeve.

The commander of the Air Force Eastern Test Range—Colonel Oscar Payne at Patrick AFB—made it clear he wanted me back for a Major's assignment within his own purview.

I took command of Antigua Air Station, West Indies, late in June 1977. And indeed, it was a dream – a glorious job on many levels – an Air Force command coupled with wide ranging diplomatic duties and insights.

"Cocktails, anyone?"
Queen Elizabeth II and Prince Phillip.

The British were shutting down their last Caribbean island colonies at the end of their 350-year empire. We participated firsthand in the unfolding of radical political and cultural change as Antigua prepared to become an independent nation. Our typical professional contacts and house guests included ambassadors, consular officials, premiers, British governors, prime ministers, ship captains, admirals, British knights, General Officers and Colonels *and* Jeannie and I were presented to Queen Elizabeth II at a cocktail party aboard HMY Britannia during her visit. I, a lowly Major.

HMY Britannia in daylight

That first summer I even was an honorary judge at the Eastern Caribbean steel band competition!

At Antigua, in Jeannie's consistent, unyielding charity in high social occasions and in daily life, I began to sense that I was married to a truly holy woman. She exhibited equal charm and solicitude to the most and least socially notable, toward the highest government officials and to our maid, to our elderly half-blind gardener, to the fishermen that brought live lobster to our kitchen door and to the school children who asked for rides into town. I have written extensively about all this in other books: *Paradise Commander* and *Saint Jeannie's Shiny Black Shoes*.

During those two magical years, Shannon began schooling at Mrs. Wimbourne's Studio Tutorial—on the British system—and Katie began to follow in her mamma's footsteps as best a two-year-old can. I have a picture of Katie standing on a chair, washing dishes at the sink.

As for me, in mid-November 1978—the year of three Popes—came the answer to that first and only prayer offered up in an

Alaskan winter. It came in a way impossible to anticipate; that the Lord of the Universe would directly, audibly speak to a clueless agnostic. And that *That Voice* would be heard five times in a four-year span. Such things, one would have thought, were reserved for well-established, great Saints. Not for a self-centered, young agnostic Major. Many are the documented records of Saints' mystical encounters with the Transcendent realm. But me?

The first incident came one month to the day after John Paul II ascended to the throne of Peter. It was a simple, audible question posed to me when I was alone on a Saturday morning. With a hint of a masculine chuckle *That Voice* said, "Why don't you pretend to believe and see what happens?" That was all. It was not just a question, considering that hint of humor, it was a dare! I took it on. After eleven years with a faithful Catholic wife, I was fully capable of *pretending* to be a faithful, praying, church going Catholic Christian. So, I did. For two weeks, I did.

And then, multiple miracles began to occur. My worldview changed at the end of November 1978.

During that two weeks of pretend belief, Jeannie was planning a last-Saturday-of-the-month sixth birthday pool party for Shannon, our first daughter. Thirty ankle biters were invited. Jeannie and our maid, Dorsett Lincoln, would handle the inside operation; bake the cake and cookies, supervise and assist clothes changing, sooth and cure six-year-old battle damage and direct parent and guest traffic.

Jeannie wanted me to handle the outside operation at the pool; decorate the pool patio, set up tables and chairs, cook and serve endless American hot dogs (bratwurst to brats, I thought) and ice cream (rare commodities on the island), umpire arguments and fish drowning kids out of the pool.

The old me mightily resisted the pro-posed tasks until I realized that even a pretend Christian would be more cooper-ative. I capitulated. OK. I'll do it, don't want to, but OK.

The rainy season was late that year but arrived with monsoonal vengeance on the Monday before the party. Absolutely continuous all that week, consistent with the air base forecast for continual rain throughout the northeast Caribbean. Yes, it rained continuously all week as worried mothers began calling, "Aren't you going to cancel the party?" These motherly calls went on all day every day right into Saturday morning. Jeannie's constant response was, "No, it won't rain, bring the children." My repeating pretend prayer was "Lord, you know I don't want to be bothered with that party, but let's do it for the children."

With rain continuing well into Saturday morning, I laid down my final appeal. "Lord, the party is scheduled from 1:00pm to 4:30pm. I need an hour for the water to run off the yard and an hour to set up outside. So, if it does not stop raining by 11:00, I *will* cancel the party. Now, come on! Let's do it for the children!" The rain continued to pour. Finally...

Jeannie and I stood at the front screen door watching the steady rain dance on the front walk. As the second hand on my

Accutron watch came around and approached my deadline hour, I counted down the seconds. "10, 9, 8, ..." At three I opened the door and stepped out on the porch. Two, one; at zero I stepped out on the front walk. The rain stopped. Exactly 11:00am! Exactly as asked in my last prayerful appeal. I was standing in ankle deep water, but not a drop fell on me.

BUT! It was raining all around our yard in every direction, all over the island and out to sea. And that was the way it was all afternoon. Rain all around us, up close and personal, but not on our yard. Two hours later, the party began on dry ground. What was going on? All the parents who brought and retrieved kids saw what I saw.

From a totally overcast sky, rain squalls processed in train on southeasterly trade winds. Most unnerving, less than a quarter mile to windward dark rain clouds were splitting like waves cut by the bow of a ship, passing barely around our yard and recombining at the beach road out in front of our house. The rain was held off our yard until....

Precisely 4:30pm; exactly. That was the time I prayed the party would end. Now, even on our yard, it rained continuously for several more days. *"Why don't you pretend to believe and see what happens?"*

Spiritual blindness was lifted. For months thereafter, even years later in some cases, we witnessed, sometimes *participated* in miraculous healings. I was directed to the Catholic Church the day after the rain incident and heard *That Voice* a second time a week later—and we encountered an angel at a midnight mass on Christmas that same year, 1978, during a visit to Houston. How did that happen?

In a Christmas visit to my mother at Houston, we discovered a large Catholic Church in the neighborhood. We decided to go to midnight Mass. The attendant urged us, "Be sure to get here at least an hour early; the churched will be packed!" Delayed by two sleepy little girls, we arrived exactly at midnight. To say the church was packed would be insufficient.

The whole church: pews, center and side aisles, back wall and vestibule were crowded almost to suffocation! Jeannie, carrying

Katie, was the last one in. I with Shannon stood teetering on the outer threshold of the church. Both children were sound asleep.

Finally, I got my balance; heels on that outer threshold. Prayer time! "Lord, the children can't see, much less hear" (over the noise of the crowd).

Immediately, I saw a bald-headed usher, way down front in the center aisle, right in front of the altar. He started elbowing and pushing his way up the center aisle. Somehow, I was assured he was coming for us. Lost sight of him, but a few minutes later, there he was, at the inner door of the vestibule looking directly at me. He elbowed his way up nose to nose with me and said, "I have four seats down front. Would you like them?" We would!

He turned without another word and started elbowing and shoving his way back into the main church with us in hot pursuit. Left across the back wall, right down the left wall, right across the front wall and up on the altar stage, pushing and elbowing all the way.

There were two rows of folding chairs set up on the stage alongside the altar. The four nearest the altar, two or three steps away, still were unoccupied. The baldheaded usher motioned that we should sit. Then disappeared. Nothing dramatic. No puff of smoke, no startling flash of light. He just was not there. Besides the disappearance, here are a few other questions with no definitive answer.

How could I have seen him so clearly in the crush of the crowd between the altar and the outer threshold of the vestibule? How is it that at the end of my one liner prayer he instantly started moving and that when he started moving, I knew without doubt he was coming for us? How could he have seen us from his post in front of the altar? There was no time for a message to be sent forward. Cell phones were yet to be invented. How could he know that in the time it took to get to us and return to the altar stage, no one else would have taken those seats? The crowd was along the front wall as well and those seats were right there in plain view. Finally, how is it that a bald headed, middle-age usher could disappear? He was right beside us, between Jeannie and I, and then he wasn't.

After that Christmas holiday, we returned to Antigua where I was baptized in January 1979.

+

Mid-February 1979. After Shannon and Katie left the supper table, Jeannie, with a little difficulty in choosing words said, "Something really strange happened to me, recently. I really don't understand it, but here, read this book."

Her demeanor was a little strange. My first thought was that she must have a life-threatening disease. But she assured me it was a good thing, just could not find the words to describe it. I went to the living room and began to read the small paperback book, *Fire on the Earth,* she offered. It was a compelling read which I finished in bed about 10pm that evening. Jeannie already was asleep.

When the day of Pentecost had come...suddenly from heaven there came a sound like the rush of a violent wind, and it filled the house.... Divided tongues, as of fire...appeared among them.... All of them were filled with the Holy Spirit and began to speak in other languages, as the Spirit gave them ability. Acts 2: 1-4

The manifestation and fire of the Holy Spirit came, following my request in prayer, near midnight on 17 February, 1979, two weeks after my baptism...

I awoke with a start. I already was praying aloud, speaking rapidly in a strange language. Fully awake, immediately I knew what was happening. I couldn't move. Paralyzed (!) but not afraid. While the audible tongues continued, a quick mental inventory revealed that I could think, hear, voice the tongues (though I had no control of that), feel and move my eyes; but could not move my head, arms, legs or torso. There was the sound of wind roaring through the house (the trade winds were calm that night) and I felt like I was burning up. This went on for two or three minutes; then the tongues started tapering off. It just went of its own accord. It was over; the tongues, the paralysis, the wind, the heat. I had full faculties.

In the morning I learned that Jeannie had had a similar encounter of the Holy Spirit weeks earlier. I gave her a full account of my experience. I said, "It was as though He held me in his arms as you would hold a baby on its back, while the Holy Spirit rewired my computer! Yesterday I was self-centered, today I am other-centered." Rewired my computer? Not said in esoteric theological terms, but considering my background at the time, it was a pretty good analogy.

Jeannie was delighted. It was then, after a little more discussion, we vowed unconditional obedience to the expressed will of God. No other life course seemed logical. His expressed will for us came readily, thereafter. But not all at once.

X

The Re-sail

Steel Wall, Evil Moon, Sunday Rising

Man's mind cannot grasp the causes of events in their completeness, but the desire to find the causes is implanted in one's soul.

Tolstoy (1828-1910)

Jeannie, my wife, had a dream before we arrived at our new posting at Andrews AFB, Maryland. She "saw" the house we later found and almost bought out in the Maryland countryside. But that dream somehow disturbed her. A fellow officer confirmed her feelings, saying, "In the natural order of USAF assignments, you likely would later move to the Pentagon. That house location made for an impossible commute in greater Washington traffic. In another dream shortly thereafter, she "saw" the apartment that the housing office eventually assigned us on base. She had not been in that area of the base.

(Our tour there *was* cut short. The proposed house purchase out in the Maryland countryside would have presented multiple problems on a quick turnaround.)

We moved in on base, placing Shannon in a Maryland public grade school on base. Catherine, now three, remained at home; literally following in her mom's footsteps. Later that first week at work, I got a very excited call from Jeannie.

"They're lilacs, Al, they're lilacs!" Six huge bushes out the kitchen door blocked the sidewalk. Her intent that morning had been to whack 'em down.

Jeannie was a Seattle girl. Up there, lilacs grow like weeds. Little girl Jeannie grew up with lilacs all around her, her favorite flower. But in Maryland? We never noticed any other lilacs during our two-year stay. The presence of lilacs, following the prophetic dreams, assured us that we were right where the Lord wanted us

At the edge of that housing area there was a gentle slope that lead down through a wooded area, across a small foot bridge over a creek and back up through more woods into the large clearing that was the main base. Already, the HQ building was in sight, but halfway there was the base chapel. I stopped in there most days on the walk back home.

The base chapel served several denominations. The Catholic tabernacle was housed in a tiny chapel off the hallway between the main chapel and the offices. It would be packed with only 20 souls. The only light in there came from the candle in a deep red glass and one dark, stained glass window behind the tabernacle. It was a very quiet place to de-compress from a day's work.

One evening in particular, I entered, closed the door and sat down in deep quiet. A few minutes later *That Voice* spoke for the third time in a couple of years: "*Do you love me?*"

Now, I wish I could report that, *immediately*, I replied with St Peter's answer, "Yes, Lord, I love you." Instead, I thought, "I've read the book. I know what's coming next!" *Then*, I said, "Yes, Lord, I love you."

That Voice said, *"Prostrate yourself."*

"WHAT?!"

THUNDERING SILENCE. Never before or since have I not heard such overwhelming silence, deeper than any cave I have been in: a Presence felt in awesome silence. "But, Lord, someone might come in!" (The whole idea suggested potential embarrassment. As a new Catholic, I hardly had seen or heard of such a thing!) More THUNDERING SILENCE. "Lo-orrd?!" I could hear a few people walking up and down the hall. Someone certainly *could* come in. "But, Lo-ord! Well, alright!"

And, so, I did. Nose to the carpet in front of the tabernacle. After what seemed a lingering eternity of prayer mixed with self-conscious listening to footsteps in the hall, and wondering what would come next, *That Voice* said, *"Go in peace."*

+

While there at Andrews AFB, we bought another sailboat; we kept Jabberwocky II, a 28-foot Bristol, at Annapolis. When we transferred back to Patrick AFB for the third time, on short orders, I called up friend Bob Wilfong from Florida. Bob had been a close friend and civilian coworker at Patrick AFB during our first and second tour there. This third time, we knew he would be working for me. He gladly came up and we sailed Jabberwocky II south. Nearly got killed, all of us—Bob, Jeannie, Shannon, Catherine and I—before we cleared Chesapeake Bay.

I don't mean metaphorically; I mean the dead kind of being killed. We left Annapolis in the afternoon, turned south on the Baltimore channel late in the day. Soon dark, we were sailing along on a broad reach in gentle airs, three or four knots. Bob was in the cockpit with me; he was at the tiller. My family was "safely" asleep below. Around 2am I began to feel a little queasy. Not exactly sick, but as if something was wrong. The feeling in my gut was increasing. Finally, I thought I heard something, turned to look back.

In moonless darkness, there was a bow light well above us at 45 degrees, and a rolling wave coming up our stern. Between the two, I was staring at the bow edge of a ship! A big freighter, riding high, fast and empty. There was no time to discuss the subject. I reached over, shoved the tiller into Bob's stomach, and we left the channel as a wall of steel slid by us. It was too quick. There was no time for fear. It was so close my only thought was, "Don't touch it; it will scratch my finger."

We circled back into the channel right behind her churning props, tips barely breaking the surface. Watching those props depart at three times our speed, I understood: they were transmitting their sound through the water below the threshold of hearing. The fiberglass hull of my boat was acting like a speaker at maybe 12 cps. Couldn't hear it, but my queasy-ness had been caused by my gut vibrating at slowly increasing amplitude as the ship approached. If we had been on a wooden boat, likely I would never have had that queasy warning.

+

Back at Patrick AFB one last time, I went to work as the Chief, Plans and Requirements for the Air Force Eastern Test Range; the long-range planning shop. Over at the base chapel, with Major Pete and his wife Joan, we established and managed a youth group program. In that church occurred a most dramatic miracle.

On a Sunday during communion I held the cup, serving a line of parishioners. When she was still two back in the line, I recognized a neighbor who lived on base a block away from us. She looked devastated. Everything about her face said fear and trembling, deep dread to the threshold of hopelessness. Then she was right before me. At the instant she touched the cup, a launch of energy taking no longer than it would take to say "Huh!" went from my entire body, a movement of Spirit. It was Power.

Perhaps you know the gospel passage. Jesus is in a crowd. A woman touches his robe. *Then Jesus asked, "Who touched me?" When all denied it, Peter said, "Master, the crowds surround you and press in on you." But Jesus said, "Someone touched me; for I*

noticed that power had gone out from me."
(Lk 8:44-46)

I am not Jesus, but that event revealed
He was in me, and I in Him, as Scripture
promises all who follow (obey) Him. (John
14:18-23). He was with me and using me in
my commitment and vow of obedience.

A week or so later, the rest of the story
was told to me. That Friday afternoon, in a
physical breast examination by her doctor, a
rather significant lump was found. The
doctor was sure, it was a cancer; she should
return on Monday for a confirming biopsy.
How far had it advanced? The fear of cancer
was on her mind as she came to the cup on
Sunday. The next day, Monday immediately
after the communion "event", she reported
to the doctor for the biopsy. No lump was
there or anywhere! There was nothing to
biopsy!

+

And as you might expect, we continued to
sail at every opportunity. On a triangle race
offshore at Daytona, crewing as navigator
for friend Ron Tyre on his boat, I won the

race for him as all the other navigators followed the lead boat, a 55-foot Hunter. The Hunter's compass was off by five degrees to the right, I assume, leading the fleet too far to sea. We made the last turn first by a mile and raced back to victory at the yacht club.

I even crewed one year in the Daytona-Bermuda race. We were on the smallest boat and finished at the middle of the pack on corrected time. Not bad for a boat, owner and crew who had never sailed a blue water race.

Our navigation was as crude as it gets. We sailed in the general direction of Bermuda, compensating for the Gulf Stream by guess and when we thought we might be within sixty or so miles of the island, turned on our hand-held FM radio with a directional antenna. Worked like a charm! The Bermuda station popped up 30 degrees off the port bow. We sailed straight into the harbor from sixty miles out!

+

Not all adventures occur under sail. This happened before our eyes on Grand Bahama

Island. The telling of this incident speaks to the depths and heights to which the human spirit may descend and ascend.

On a Friday night, Bob Wilfong, Jeannie and I sailed across the Gulf Stream on his boat, entered the Grand Bahama bank at dawn, Saturday, and sailed across in eight feet of crystal-clear water to Marsh harbor. Bob's wife Jodi was 9 months pregnant, so she flew over and met us at the dock in the late afternoon.

At Marsh Harbor, we tied up close inshore at the Conch Restaurant. The conch supper at sunset was a delight— accompanied by drinks and comradely laughter on the patio; but under the glare of a single light bulb hanging from the roof corner nearest the dock, night on the boat seemed to stretch endlessly in the tropic heat. The mosquitos buzzed Tora, Tora! Tora! in relentless attack above the forward hatch screen while I lay sweating, drowsing on the left V berth.

Sometime after midnight, I was jolted completely awake by shouts and feet thumping the dock boards in haste, running past our bow and out toward the far end of the dock. That single, finger dock stuck out 30 yards onto the Grand Bahama bank, hosting a few boats in side-slips closer in. The remainder of the narrow dock, without side slips, reached out into the gloom of night fog. There was room out there in deeper water for a vessel to dock alongside. Faintly, I still could hear the men at the sea end of the dock, but they were speaking a Bahamian dialect that I could not follow. Then another ran by us, then a fourth, shouting in the same dialect.

Then it got quiet, really quiet, with only the gentle slap of wavelets tapping the bow under my berth. Curiosity and the desire for a cooling breeze got the better of me. I struggled up through the forward hatch into a cloud of mosquitoes, reattached the screen and stepped over the bow pulpit onto the dock.

It was dark out there at the far end, well away from that glaring light bulb. The moon provided little light, straining through high thin clouds. Fog drifted across, growing thicker with each step. I could see the slightest shadow outline of a person leaning on the last piling to seaward. But four men had run out there! Where were the other three? No telling what I was getting myself into, so I approached with deliberate caution.

There was a middle-aged woman there in a nightgown, holding on to that last piling like a long-lost friend. She spoke to me with a pronounced slur. "'e discherved it," she said; "'e discherved evvrar bit uvf it." I followed her gaze to the right and down to the aft deck of their cabin cruiser lying alongside. The four Bahamians were down there, struggling to center a corpulent, middle-aged man on a filthy, blood soaked 4'x 6' rug. The object of their struggle has fallen drunk, face down, *very* out cold. The woman assured me again that he descherved "it", evvvraer bit uvf it!

I chose to keep her company. Another person down there would just be in the way. Finally, the quartet lifted their bloody load to the dock. Regaining their footing, they lifted the corpus laden rug and began a slow, foggy procession up the dock to a waiting ambulance, with me bringing up the rear. The woman stayed, hugging her friend the dock piling, but as we processed toward land, I heard her whisper one more time, "He descherved it, he descherved evvar' bit uvf it."

I never learned what "it" was that he did, but she? After he passed out face down on the deck, she found the butcher knife in the galley drawer, carved off his right buttock, and chummed the Bahamian waters.

It was an evil moon, but 'e was a lucky mon 'e was, I say. Aye, 'e was a lucky mon. Wha' if 'e lay on 'is back, I say. Wha' then, matey, Eh? Wha' then?

+

A glorious golden Sunday morning sky smiled on Marsh Harbor. Other than the cabin cruiser riding gentle waves at the end of the dock, there was no evidence of what the long night had seen.

We went ashore to inquire if a church was nearby. The dock master said, "Follow them. They know the way." He called to a Bahamian family in their dialect as they were departing. Happily, they waved us in among them with big smiles. We were welcomed as long-lost friends. And we *were* friends – of the same Lord.

We walked up a shell road leading into the palmettos, scattered palms and pines behind the marina. Ambling up the road, they began to sing familiar sounding spiritual songs interspersed with joyful patois commentary, impromptu dancing, clowning among the young, and laughter. Other families joined from side paths as we progressed; more families taking up the song and dance as the congregation doubled and redoubled. After no more than a mile of singing and dancing up the road, our crowd rounded a sharp corner to the right; revealing a classic unpainted little steeple-d country church tucked away in a clearing.

We stopped, awaiting a priest and a key. The Bahamians tried and we tried to converse with little success; it was mostly point and name and smile and shake hands. The singing picked up again, a little individual dancing and the priest arrived --- also Bahamian.

We crowded in, choosing a bench three or four from the back. The interior offered bare plank benches, walls and flooring. No statues, no pictures, no glass windows; only louvered shutters which they opened. Only the altar revealed traces of faded paint. The congregation filled the tiny church as the congregants settled down in prayerful anticipation.

The mass began, with boisterous singing in the same patois, punctuated by raised hands and praise. At the start of the homily, an infant to our right started to cry, quite loud. What the mother did was... well... never seen before by us. She handed the crying baby to the person on her left.

That person passed the baby to the left as before. And to the next, and .... The process continued back and forth on every row in the church. After a few passes the baby stopped crying—became entranced by the changing faces—and by the end of the homily everyone, including us palefaces, had held that quietened baby that eventually was returned to its mother. The mass continued without interruption.

After the mass, the coming to Jesus reversed: singing as we returned; laughing, dancing and waving goodbye as one by one, families split off on one path or another through the palmettos, palms and pines to return to their huts. Finally, we were alone again at dockside, in wonderment at all that we had seen and heard. This was true joy amidst grinding poverty. The poor of spirit shall, really do, see God now and in the kingdom to come.

Masses are the same on each particular Sunday world-wide, only varying in vernacular, as I had learned years earlier in French Martinique; but never before or since have we encountered such joy in the midst of poverty, such joy in receiving Christ. Except, perhaps, in the local Mexican barrio parish here, to which we were welcomed as long-lost friends in our elder years.

We left the Marsh Harbor dock late that same morning and set sail North across the Bahama Bank toward Man-O-War Cay, accompanied by three waterspouts dancing in a tight circle off to the west, off our port beam: reminders of the joyful dancing we witnessed on the road to Calvary.

XI

The Unwilling – Mystical Obedience

They who have my commandments and keep them are those who love me; and those who love me will be loved by my Father, and I will love them and reveal myself to them.
John 14: 21 NRSV

From the chapter title you might surmise that I was unwilling to do something. Well, yes and no. And to avoid potential misunderstanding, a clear definition has to be offered before we proceed. We will not be writing about a half-naked old man sitting cross legged on a mountain top humming the name of a pagan god (an unsightly thought). That is the popular view. However...

A "practical" character and an "objective" cast of mind are characteristic marks of the Christian mystic. ...he may be called a mystic who is contemplative in any religious sense; an acute "awareness" of God and his activities and manifestations being the essence of mysticism.

A Catholic Dictionary. Donald Attwater, Gen. Ed; see "Mysticism" p 337.

At the time we expressed our vows of unconditional obedience to the living God, (Chapter IX) we could not have known the fullness of consequence. All we knew was that God wanted the best for his own—and we *wanted* to be His own. Total, unconditional obedience was the logical stance; the opposite could not lead to anything really good since the Lord already had made his presence known so dramatically in word and action; already was revealed to us in our beginning mystical awareness. We wanted more—all of it! We just did not know what that entailed.

We did not know until years later that Saint Jane Frances de Chantal, religious, had it all figured out. She described the consequences of a vow of unconditional obedience to her nuns, as recorded by her secretary.

"...there is another martyrdom; the martyrdom of love. Here God keeps his servants ...in this present life so that they may labor for him, and he makes of them both martyrs and confessors. By the favor of God, some (are)...more fortunate than others in that their desire has been granted, will actually suffer such a martyrdom. One sister asked what form this martyrdom took.

"The saint answered: 'Yield yourself fully to God, and you will find out! Divine love takes its sword to the hidden recesses of our inmost soul and divides us from ourselves, just as completely and effectively as if a tyrant's blade had severed spirit from body. (This will last) from the moment when we commit ourselves unreservedly to God, until our last breath.'"

Vol. I, Liturgy of the Hours, Proper of
Saints, Dec 12.

How did this all play out in our lives? How was I "cut off from all that was dearest to me" as Saint Jane expressed it? "Just as completely and effectively as if a tyrant's blade had severed spirit from body"? Furthermore, I had professed love by prostration. *They who have my commandments and keep them are those who love me.* Would I persevere? At Patrick AFB, late in 1982, I found out what Saint Jane and Jesus meant. The real test of my love of God came due.

Early retirement from the Air Force seemed the right thing to do despite my strong personal will to remain in the profession I so loved. After long years of dedication to the mission, it seemed that I was the Air Force and the Air Force was me. My whole self-identity was at risk. I could not retire. I had no will to retire. I would not retire. Yet, unconditional obedience and call to perseverance seemed due. (I have explained why in *Paradise Commander*.)

My secretary had taken the day off. Behind her desk she had a typing table set against the wall, holding the only typewriter in the office (PCs were still in the future). I sat down and typed my letter of resignation and request for retirement. I swiveled around to the left, put my feet up on her desk; staring at that letter held in my right hand. I said, half aloud, "Are you really going to sign that letter?" The secretary's phone rang.

It was Marion, my former secretary at Andrews AFB. We slipped right into the same old familiar chit chat. I had not moved; feet on desk, letter in right hand, staring at that letter while talking. *Staring at that letter while talking.*

In the middle of a sentence, Marion's voice dropped an octave, went masculine and *That Voice* said, "I know you are trying to make a difficult decision, and I want you to go ahead and do it." Marion's voice immediately returned to normal. Told what I had heard, she said, "My God!"

I said, "Yes, I think so." There was nothing left to say. We said goodbye and I signed the letter. *Divine love ...divides us from ourselves.*

XII

The Teaching – A Mission Assignment

As a rule, religious persons generally assume that whatever natural facts connect themselves in any way with their destiny are significant of the divine purpose with them... and if it be "trial," strength to endure the trial is given. (I)n the process of communion energy from on high flows in to meet demand and becomes operative within the phenomenal world...whether its immediate effects be subjective or objective.

William James, Philosopher, Psychologist *Varieties of Religious Experience, (1902)*

I retired early from the USAF, effective the end of May 1983. The decision plunged me into another bout of depression, but I had vowed obedience and in prostration, nose to the carpet, had professed love of God. There was no turning back. The will of the Lord was clear.

It later became clear that we were going to Seattle, Jeannie's family home, where I was to attend Seattle University. How did we know that? William James describes the process above, but here are the specifics in our case.

With the resignation signed and delivered, the clock started ticking toward the effective date, 31 May. I had a family to support and no job prospects. I had never looked around to consider alternatives; why should I? I was the Air Force! The Air Force was me! Resignation terrified me! Oh, my God! Obedience is painful! But, *thy will be done....*

The Lord will provide.... But he does seem to enjoy the cliff hanger. After several months of worry between the signing and effective dates, probably in March 1983, I arrived home at our base quarters after work to find Jeannie at the door. "Here, read this; no not that; read that little ad." It offered a Master of Pastoral Ministry at Seattle University – all the way across the country from Patrick AFB in Jeannie's hometown. Was that God's will for us?

I called Dr. Leo Stanford, Ph.D., head of the program. He responded with a pile of forms to fill out and a choice to be made. From a list of 50 options, I had to choose a practicum. The whole list bored me. Were there any other options? No. But there was one item I did not understand. The RCIA. I asked. He explained.

"RCIA stands for Rite of Christian Initiation for Adults. It is a new initiative in the Catholic Church for the education of converts. You are a convert. This might be of interest to you. You would be teaching and guiding other converts."

"Sign me up! God provides!" Just barely. I would have a monthly retirement check and the GI bill. Seattle University threw in a few extra bucks and a small tuition discount. But the cost of living was higher on the west coast. We could survive with care. Lots of care.

We bought a motor home, toured the nation all that summer and I signed in at Seattle University the end of August. It was a needed break from all the worry about what was next. At least we thought we knew what the next year would bring. And the kids loved the travel. In two months, we drove 6,000 miles, averaging 100 miles a day, back and forth sig zag-ing north and south, but ever westward from Florida to Seattle.

Memories? Shannon riding a horse in Tennessee, seeing my paternal grandmother for the last time at Lafayette, Louisiana, Catherine at the Colorado Springs Zoo, exploring an old frontier fort in Wyoming, and our two cats. At every stop they needed to use the "facilities." But we could not let them run free. So, Jeannie put them both on the same leash. Cats never cooperate with one another, will not decide on the same direction. They never got more than 50 feet from the motor home.

Arriving at Seattle, we sold the motor home and settled in, first with Jeannie's sister, then in a rental house up the hill. Signed both girls into the neighborhood Catholic school. The school was well run, but the students were extremely provincial and like all children, could be cruel.

In a geography lesson, the teacher was showing the class maps and describing the eastern Caribbean. When she mentioned Antigua, Shannon said, "I've been there!" All the class told her she was a liar. She came home crying. In another class Katie brought a large black slug in a jar to show and tell. All the kids ridiculed her. This time, the teacher caught it and used the occasion to teach the class that not all the world had Seattle black slugs and that Katie had been many places where there were none. Katie came home crying from that one, too.

Meanwhile, Jeannie made time to feed and console Seattle's street children while running a household and raising two daughters. But adults can be cruel, too. Jeannie staged a wonderful little party to celebrate Katie's first communion. None of Jeannie's half dozen or so Seattle relatives came. Katie cried, again.

The classes at Seattle University were right up my alley: surveys of theology, psychology, ethics, counseling, and behavioral dynamics analysis in class and in sub-group interactions among fellow students. All this applied to my practicum, the Rite of Catholic Initiation for Adults. And it was in the practicum experienced as a team member in a Bellevue church 'cross Lake Seattle that I began to understand and appreciate the liturgical processes of the Catholic Church. And, not mentioned in the University catalogue, the whole process I went through also was an intensive, sometimes painful course of self-discovery. But angst over my retirement began to subside.

Neither angst nor self-discovery would end there, but a firm foundation was set for the personal edifice the Lord later would build in me. I had no clue that eventually the Lord would mold of me an accomplished catechist, retreat master, author and spiritual director. I just was following my nose in hopes that I would not stray too far from the will of God.

The Air Force career I so loved could not have lasted forever, nor could the Master's program. Classes would come to an abrupt end early in June 1984, and once again I had no prospects. But we were—painfully—

learning to wait upon the Lord, the Lord who loved the cliff hanger. Meanwhile, the landlord knew my program was ending and he was urging us to get out. He had a prospect in waiting.

+

It was morning, a Tuesday. I was getting up late at eight with a class starting at nine all the way across traffic choked Seattle. The phone rang. Exasperated, I answered, "Hello?!" Short pause.

Then a voice, not *That Voice,* said, "Can you be on a plane at 11:00 o'clock this morning?"

"Sure," I said, "Where is it going?" Longer pause; mild laughter.

"My secretary took the day off, and I hardly know what I am doing! This is Tony Rodriguez, personal director for Federal Electric Corporation at Vandenberg AFB, CA. We would like to talk with you. Can you make the plane? I'll pick you up in Santa Maria." I did and he did.

I was interviewed by David Little, whom I knew from a meeting during my first tour at Patrick AFB in 1965; and by Joan Anderson, still a friend after all these years. It was Joan's task, also, to take me back to the airport.

Somewhere along the way I said, "Joan, I don't understand. All day it felt like I was interviewing you and Dave, not the other way around."

"Don't you know?"

"Don't I know what?"

"We were told to hire you!" (God really *does* provide! I had not applied for a job there. They came and got me anyway.)

"Really?!" So, what happens now?"

"Go home and wait. Tony will call you with an offer from Dave, another from me. Pick the one you like and come on down!"

I went to work with Dave in long range planning for the Western Test Range, preparing the range to support ballistic missile and satellite polar launches; the same type of work I had done for Air Force Systems Command and the Eastern Test Range my last four years of active duty.

We settled in Santa Maria, bought a house and joined St Louis de Montfort Parish. The girls were signed into Catholic schools. They both were destined to graduate from High School in Santa Maria. Jeannie, among many other activities, ran a bible study group for the ladies, ministered to incarcerated teens and took meals to homebound, terminal HIV patients awaiting death. Oh! And at least one more thing I was not prepared for.

I arrived home from work one day to hear crashing and banging going on. Walked into the kitchen and found my delicate little spouse with sledgehammer in hand, demolishing the kitchen. "I want a new kitchen," she said. Like Lola in the song, Jennie gets what she wants!

I did not rush into pastoral work—for a year, I concentrated on my new job. It paid off. I was promoted to branch chief, then department manager in just over a year. But something was left hanging. My class requirements had been completed, but there was a report of in-the-field work due to complete my practicum. Busy at work, I stalled for that first year. Besides, there was no RCIA program at St. Louie de Montfort where I could begin to participate. Then....

On a Sunday, I sat down at home after mass to read the parish bulletin. I saw it before I could get comfortable in the easy chair; a tiny little article that said:

"Anyone interested in starting an RCIA program, please attend a Wednesday meeting with Father Anthony in the rectory dining room at 8:30pm."

I went. As soon as I admitted my Seattle University experience, I was named Director and the meeting was adjourned.

+

In seven years, we had come from afar in obedience to the Lord's leadings; given in voice and circumstance through his periodic revelation of presence, will, healing and divine love. We committed ourselves unreservedly through the many twists and turns in our lives. The Lord fully prepared us for the RCIA assignment, delivered us to Santa Maria, provided our fiscal needs and this opportunity as well. So, Director I would be.

Throughout, Jeannie was right there; spouse, friend, spiritual counselor, agent of hospitality and protocol advisor. She had her own mission as well: everywhere serving the sick and elderly, teaching and consoling street children and incarcerated youths. Together in the Spirit, we experienced St Paul's list of gifts, from teaching to tongues. These gifts are palpable, real. Not given continuously, but present in response to the needs of the moment.

Now you are the body of Christ and individually members of it. And God has appointed in the Church first apostles, second prophets, third teachers: then deeds of power, then gifts of healing, forms of assistance, forms of leadership, various kinds of tongues.

1 Cor 12:27,28 NRSV

We lived and worked in Santa Maria for seventeen years. We organized and I directed and taught RCIA. Jeannie managed hospitality and lead group discussions. As a retreat master of a separate program and team we founded sixteen small prayer communities in the parish.

During this same period, we associated with the Benedictine Monastery of the Risen

Christ at San Luis Obispo. After several years of study with Abbot David and his community, I graduated from their School for Spiritual Directors. Jeannie also attended most of the classes given during various retreats conducted at Valyermo, a monastery across the mountains north of Pasadena, CA.

But at Vandenberg AFB we were in slow decline. The Russians gave up their empire on Christmas day, 1989. The Supreme Soviet granted themselves free air travel on Aeroflot for a year and hauled down the Soviet flag for the last time.

During 1990, the Air Force started cutting back on our contracts, bit by bit. I laid off a lot of good people during and after 1991, knowing my own number was certain to come up sooner or later as the cutting continued. Industries have their own cruel ways. They waited until I was on a religious retreat to sever my management position as department manager, though they did keep me on in more or less temporary marketing positions for another year.

When the layoff came, my manager at the time, an alcoholic, could not face me; so, he left a note on my desk to "report to personnel" when I was down the hall. He then took a two-week vacation. The personnel director at the time, was furious at him, but I had my two-week notice.

At the beginning of those dark days Shannon compounded the suffering in the family. She kicked over the traces, rebelled, turned her back on personal responsibility, God, church, education and family; at seventeen went her own sordid way into darkness.

And Catherine? Psychologists often have observed that when the first child abdicates the natural rights and duties of sibling order, the second child will step up and assume the role. Catherine (who repented of her own lesser mistakes) went on to graduate on the Dean's list at Seaton Hall. She is the former assistant director at a Montessori school and is following, no, exceeding her father in evangelical works as a core member of a strong group that conducts healing masses on a global basis. Their audiences often number in the tens of thousands (!) from Western Borneo to California and back to Manila.

XIII

The Pause and Re-training – A Reboot

The midlife crisis is that by the time you find out who you is, it's who you was!
                                    The Author

Retirement came the second time in 1995. Not my choice, but at least at age 55 there was a partial pension attached. Before we get into what next, one more pre-retirement sub-vignette, if that's a word. You may not know this, but a world record was established at San Luis Obispo, CA, during the early '90s. Engineering students at Cal Poly accomplished a long thought impossible engineering feat. Man-powered helicopter flight! How do I know? I was there.

Mid-afternoon at my desk I got a call from my friend and former boss, the Personnel Director. He had received a call from a Cal Poly professor saying they were going to attempt a world record flight that same evening. They needed an independent, qualified certifying witness. Could we help? My name came up immediately: a retired USAF officer with cruise missile engineering test experience – a test planning manager – a dependable straight shooter. Could I get up there and help?

I drove up and reported in at the basketball gym shortly after dark. After brief pleasantries, a faculty member led me up into the bleachers overlooking mid-court. He was trying to give me instructions, but I was awestruck at that thing down on the court under the glare of gym lights.

It was almost all rotor. Four blades, each the approximate size of a Cessna 150 wing, spanned the width of the court and a little more, leaving maybe a yard either side between rotor tips and the bleacher walls. Built not of aluminum, but probably bass wood struts covered over by what appeared to be varnished paper or extra thin fabric. It was model airplane technology on a super scale. Super light! At the center, a vertical drive shaft, certainly of light-weight aluminum, reached down to a set of bicycle gears set under a racing bicycle seat. It was supported on four spindly legs, each with a tiny wheel. The whole thing was supposed to fly by the efforts of their best racing bicyclist. The students designed and built it, but this was the first time they would attempt a witnessed flight. It was all or nothing!

When he finally got my attention, the faculty member handed me a stopwatch, pen and clipboard with the certification form. For certification, the thing had to hover off the floor untouched by anyone but the "engine." (I do not remember exact requirements, but let's say a yard off the floor for one minute. Something like that.)

In the meantime, the student ground crew was fussing around, making last minute checks. When ready, one student was stationed at each rotor tip, securing a centered position on the gym floor. The potential problem, of course, was that the thing could not be steered except by the "engine" leaning one way or another, a maneuver that would rob him of significant pedal power. If it drifted left or right by a yard or so, a rotor would hit a bleacher wall.

Then the "engine" strode out of a locker room like a conquering gladiator, adjusted himself on the seat and nodded. The ground crew stepped back, and the "engine" looked up at me. I gave one thumb up and he began to pedal, gently at first. The rotor began to turn, barely at first, then a little faster, then faster. The "engine" was really hustling when two wheels lifted off the floor, bounced and settled back down. There had been barely any drift at all. The "engine" gave it his all and the thing lifted off the floor— stopwatch running.

They did it! At minimum success, I signaled the ground crew. The "engine" kept going for assurance, a little longer. Then settled the thing back on the floor. It had drifted no more than a foot in any direction. I certified minimum height and total elapsed time flown. A world record unlikely ever to be bested.

+

I worked twelve years at ITTFederal Services, until my forced retirement. I went home and told Jeannie that was it. No more aerospace. Two aerospace careers and retirements in 34 years. Enough! She was shocked, but I knew it was futile seeking another aerospace job. Good men and women still were being laid off in droves throughout the defense industry. It went on for several years.

A man's life is his work, and too often his work becomes his life. Without the familiar faces and work routines I drifted off into depression again. That Jeannie understood. She had seen it several times. She understood I needed some separation and rumination time to find a new me.

At the same time, AMTRAK and VIA were offering a one-month unlimited North American rail pass for less than $700. During the next five years I traveled by train all over the US and Canada three times, mostly in Canada from Vancouver to Halifax and as far north as Fort Churchill on Hudson's Bay and Schefferville in the extreme northwest corner of Labrador. Without recounting all the miles of staring out the train window and walking about, I will share with you, if you will allow my new word "sub-vignette," my favorite encounters along the way without regard to order of occurrence.

Fort Churchill. The train to Churchill departs Winnipeg in the early evening. If ever you make the trip, go first to the Arctic museum in town. Then you will have a greater understanding: the what and the why of what you will see.

The route starts to the west, then curves northward into Manitoba. There were in this train a baggage car, three coaches, a sleeper, café car, and another sleeper in that order. The last sleeper carried a private group on a polar bear excursion.

In coach, I was one of only three passengers. When the conductor collected my ticket, I expressed concern for the economy of three empty coaches. He suggested that I not worry; informed me that I would wake up in the morning to a train full of Indians. He was right. Not an empty seat to be found. I spent part of the morning playing hide and seek with an Indian baby over the back rest ahead. The

Indians nearby, especially the parents, watched with glee. But the real treat was the action at every Indian village stop.

Like in the old days, each Indian village turned out in the March snow. It was the big event of the day at each stop. Children were running and calling out. Mail bags were dropped off and picked up. Baggage and passengers would arrive and depart with hugs around for family members at train side. Teens on snowmobiles and barking dogs raced the departing train with evident joy.

Late afternoon we arrived at the end of the Thompson spur where most of the Indians departed: to jobs or shopping and social visits. The train was turned around on an adjacent Y track and we departed ever northward; but now, things changed.

It took the entire second night to go the 110 or so miles to Churchill. The tracks are on tenuous permafrost that could melt unexpectedly in spots. Every fifty yards there were vertical pipes stuck in the ground to radiate any warmth, to keep the ground frozen. Typical speed was 10 mph. There were times throughout the night a crewman would walk the track ahead with a flashlight, leading the diesel as though on a leash in a slow, deliberate walk. Toward early morning the pace picked up to 35 as we reached dependable permafrost. In early morning light. it was clear we were crossing the arctic tree line. An hour short of treeless Churchill, the scrub trees of the last hour took decades to reach the height of a man. Then no trees at all.

Why Churchill? I was there with snow and ice everywhere. Hudson Bay was frozen solid. Huge mounds of ice were stacked up on the beach, pushed up by frigid northern winds. It was 13 degrees that day in March and I was walking the snowy streets of a nearly deserted town all day in tennis shoes. (Dumb! Don't do that!) There was only one general store and a community center open.

I had an "incident" in the community center; wandered through several modern interconnected buildings, finding a children's room (toys all over the floor) a cafeteria, TV room, etc.' but no one in any room. Place seemed empty. Found a public rest room. Down the hall there was a janitor sweeping the floor.

I took my watch off to wash my hands, then forgot it on the shelf. As I started to leave the building I remembered and retraced my steps. No watch. It had to be the janitor. Game on.

I asked him if he had found the watch. "No". Since he was obviously of limited intelligence, I continued the game without accusation. Thanked him for his work in keeping the bathroom clean, told him if he found it, I would be in town all day. Turned and slowly pretended to leave. At which point he said he found a watch, could it be mine? It was.

I thanked him again, he handed me the watch, obviously expecting a reward. If he had been straightforward, I probably would have tipped him.

Churchill? Huge grain elevators along the shore of Hudson Bay told the tale. For a couple of summer months, people would be all over that little town. Grain ships would come and go delivering Canadian wheat the short route to northern Europe and Russia. That is why the railroad and those grain elevators.

That same evening, I re-boarded the train for the overnight walk to Thompson.

<u>Labrador</u>. The passenger train leaves Sept-Isles on the Saint Lawrence estuary early morning once each week and heads due north. The first third of the trip is among beautiful tree laden hills, occasional canyons with a nice couple of waterfalls. As the trees thin and the land flattens out to sub-arctic tundra, we stopped at a junction to drop off a couple of coaches bound west for Labrador City. Another diesel stood by at the junction to pick them up.

After de-coupling the two coaches, a crewman removed a protective derailer, we drifted through onto track clearly in less repair, still pointing due north, and he replaced and locked the derailer. Next stop, Schefflerville, arriving about 4:30pm.

Schefflerville in summer is more abandoned than Churchill in winter. The iron mines are shut down, but the government keeps a train running and essentials in the town to serve five Indian tribes in the area. (Indians – that's why there was a guard on the train, a pleasant, but armed businesslike guy that I befriended on the way up.) The housing area for the long-gone miners and their families was neat, orderly, lawns mowed and ready to move in if the mines reopened—a Canadian 'burb, but nobody home.

One man did live there in the hotel full time. He alone ran the hotel as receptionist, cashier, cook, waiter, dishwasher, bartender, bus boy, maintenance man and room cleaner. He was the sole taxi driver, tour guide and grocery clerk at the well-stocked store and filling station. I rode into town free with the guard, was given a taxi tour of housing and the store on the way and settled in for a pleasant evening meal, drink and chit chat with the guard and proprietor.

Awake at 4:30 next morning, the high latitude sun was up, and it was snowing – 24th of June. The train crew, the guard and I had a very nice bacon, 'taters and eggs breakfast at six. I asked the guard, sitting at my end of the table, "So who is up front running the train?"

As the heavy-set guy straight across the long table laughed, the guard said, "The guy straight across from you." We had a nice chat. Turns out he was from Gaspe and I had been there the week before. And I confessed that I had been a train nut from childhood.

After breakfast, I checked out of the hotel. The guard gave me a free taxi ride with him back to the train. His job was to unlock the train, start the diesel, turn on the heaters, keep out any Indians that showed up without a fare and make things ready for the crew, who came a half hour later. I sat alone in coach for about an hour before the train started to move. As it began to roll, my friend the guard walked by without stopping; said in passing, "You're wanted up front."

I followed him through the baggage car and the generator car which provided power and electric heat to the coaches (we had a freight engine up front, an SD-43 not equipped for passenger service). He opened the door. We stepped across the coupler, walked up the right outside catwalk of the slow-moving diesel in the snow, opened the cab door. The engineer barked, "Sit over there!" I rode all the way back to the Labrador City junction in the left seat of the diesel, in a minor snowstorm.

I think we gabbed all the way about his hometown Gaspe, my travels, and his experiences on the railroad; including rear ending an ore train than nearly killed him. Said it was not his fault. The train dispatcher, who was fired, had lost track of the fact there was a stopped ore train.

But this whole Schefferville story is leading up to something that happened halfway back to the junction. We were at track speed, 35mph on a long straight to the junction. Up ahead in the snow we saw three moose walking side by side, going south on the tracks. They were enjoying the shallow snow over the tracks where we had passed the day before.

We slowed to moose speed, eased up on their tails, blasted the horn and backed off maybe 50 feet. No reaction. Repeated the process and backed off. No reaction. Just three moose friends out for a pleasant morning stroll. The engineer said, "Moose are the dumbest animals on the planet. Well, I have a schedule to keep. He cranked up the power. Right on their tails the left and right moose peeled off into the deep snow. The center moose turned into mooseburger.

"Don't worry, the engineer said, "The Indians will have that moose on the fire before the meat gets cold."

Montreal. The night train to Halifax was due to leave late afternoon, but checkout time at the Marriott was noon. Having run out of things to do, I went to the train station to crowd watch and wait.

(When I checked in at the Marriott a week earlier, the clerk looked ready to throw the bum out, until I showed him my Marriott Rewards card and military ID. I said, "I'll look and smell better after a shower. Been on a train for four days." He smiled and issued my key.) Anyway, the train station.

Montreal station is to Canadian rail and bus travel what Chicago union is to the US. A grand central station. Huge does not describe the waiting room. Humongous gets closer. It takes a full five minutes just to walk normally across wall to wall. I sat on a bench near the entrance to the underground tunnel that led through downtown. I had walked all over downtown for several days, often using that tunnel.

Perusing the room and all the folks going to and fro, restaurant to train ticket booth, to bus line ticketing, to just wandering around and waiting as was I; I noticed a large man in a suit standing next to the tunnel entrance, trying to look incon-spicuous. He had the same demeanor as Secret Service guys in Washington. It was clear he was not just casually standing there. Eventually I identified three others, one near each corner of the waiting room, all trying to look casual. But despite the sunglasses, clearly, they were methodically scanning the room.

Walked over to the nearest and said, "I have noticed four of you guys at the four corners scanning the crowd. Is something going down?"

He smiled and said, quite firmly, "Go sit down, but keep watching." I thought that sounded like good advice. The four maintained their station for the next hour and a half.

As the time passed, I noticed two skinheads, big muscle building types, 230 lbs. apiece entering the waiting room. Each was carrying a very large, very full olive drab duffel bag. They sat down on a backless bench. The switchback line of bus customers who were waiting for tickets was right behind them. Military on leave? Marines?

A few minutes later, I discovered that my quartet was missing. More scanning and searching. There! They were all together in that slow-moving ticket line. Then they were behind that bench. Simultaneously, as with one mind, from the back they grabbed the skinheads, two cops apiece, lifted them head high and slammed them face down on the concrete floor. They were nose bleeding in cuffs before they could think, marched out to the bus terminal and a waiting paddy wagon.

<u>Halifax</u>. It's a big port city but was a fairly poor city when I was there. Shabby around the edges. And so was I. And tired. With my backpack, train wrinkled, worn and dirty clothes, scruffy tennis shoes and baseball hat I looked the part of a bum. And I was running short on cash. I checked in at the Y. The room was simple, cheap, the bed was clean (no bed bugs) and it had a private bathroom and shower. Feeling better, I went to take a look around. The Y's four floors and my room were a few degrees shabbier than the rest of downtown, but a large poster in the lobby promised a building renovation. I

walked the streets, got oriented and returned to the Y at dark.

The elevator creaked and groaned as though near collapse, but delivered me along with an unshaven, grizzled man of about my age (late 50's.) We both got off on the third floor, turned right and started down the hall. It immediately was clear that most of the residents were in residence. Down the far end of the hall, a thick cloud of smoke and occasional guffaws emanated from the TV room. The smoke in the hall had that unmistakable smell. As we plodded down the hall in the direction of the TV room, my accompaniment rolled a joint, slowed in the hall and offered it to me with a gentlemanly gesture.

I declined politely with thanks. He completely stopped, gave me the most soulful look of deep pity and quietly, almost painfully said, "Oh. (Short pause) You don't?!" He shook his head soulfully and continued down the hall toward the TV room. I turned left down a side hall to my room.

<u>Back to Montreal</u>. This one could have put me in the slammer. Back in Montreal I

was just about out of cash and looking more homeless every day. Need proof? I was sitting on the front steps of a neighborhood church. Even Montreal gets hot in midsummer. I put my baseball hat down on the same step, wiped my brow of sweat; closed my eyes for a moment. I heard a gentle plop. Someone going inside dropped a couple of Canadian dollars in my hat. Interesting, I thought. I continued my best to look destitute. Worked like a charm.

That Sunday, I approached the English Cathedral through a back alley. There was a little cluster of men back there, looking about as homeless as I. Stopped to chat. It became clear pretty quickly that they were a loose band of petty thieves. Interesting to talk with, so I hung around talking to their unofficial leader, who mentored me in thieving skills, especially how not to get caught.

We entered the Cathedral together and the band spread out looking for marks, ladies who might leave their purses on the bench during Communion. I sat down. My "mentor" sat two rows back. Everything went well until I went to Communion. On return to my seat, the wide eyed "mentor" clearly was having second thoughts about me. He followed me for some distance after Mass, finally dropping off. If they had been caught, they easily could have fingered me as one of their own.

All in all, I had a great time in Canada. I love Canada, Eh?

Once back home, with two monthly retirement checks and a welfare check, we began to realize that we were slowly going bankrupt. The high cost of California life, compounded by state income tax (10% of Federal tax) on our miserable income, was just too much. Once again, it seemed time for God to provide.

XIV

The Ronda Effect – Final Mission?

I perceive that I am dealt with by superior powers. This is a pleasure, a joy, an existence which I have not procured myself. I speak as a witness on the stand, and tell what I have perceived....

Thoreau

Early in 2001, again with Transcendent guidance, I accepted a job at Our Lady of Corpus Christi (OLCC); directing campus operations and maintenance, managing student work-study efforts and teaching business electives. Jeannie was quite certain that St Mary had a hand in the move, and she may have. Jeannie wrote extensive journals including her own dialog with Mary. But it happened like this.

Up in Paso Robles, CA, the story goes, three little old ladies were told they could not possibly start a Marian Eucharistic Conference in their town. Ridiculous that they should attempt such. So, they got their backs up and did it. They arranged for Nationally known priest-speakers and drew a regional crowd of 300 participants in this little one-horse town the first year, about 500 each year thereafter. A resounding success.

We attended the first three and the fifth annual event. At that fifth event, Fr Jim K____, substituting for another speaker, was hawking his start up college in Corpus Christi, Texas. At the same time, he had someone hand out tri-folds re: the college. I spoke to Fr Jim as he left the stage. He had mentioned the need for competent staff. He, in a hurry, said, "Write to me."

I did the next day. Then nothing. A few months later, I had forgotten the letter, he called me at bedtime, 1am his time. We talked for an hour and a half; followed up with an interview in Corpus Christi.

The pay was minimal, but leaving California accomplished an effective pay raise in itself. Further, social security soon would kick in as well. We could survive as middle-income Texans. It was there in Corpus Christi that we finished a 25-year avocational career with the RCIA, a work that had continued throughout the dark years of early retirement.

Adoration Chapel at Our Lady of Corpus Christi
Corpus Christi, Texas

Down the hall at OLCC there was a woman teaching philosophy. Inevitably, faculty get to know each other; as did we. Along with her teaching career Ronda Chervin, Ph.D., professor of philosophy and spirituality, has published over 60 books, mostly on various aspects of Catholic life, is a noted Catholic speaker and has been interviewed on the Eternal Word Television Network.

At OLCC, she also had a little writers' group, a half dozen or so members strong. In her enthusiasm she invited me, then encouraged me, finally resorted to nagging me at least to show up for one meeting. "And bring something!"

I wrote a few pages about my humorous encounter with a casino bouncer at Antigua, WI. The group thoroughly enjoyed my reading of it, and I realized that I "enjoy having written," as Steinbeck once said. In a word, I was hooked! This is my seventh book! (Benny the casino bouncer is the principle actor in chapter IV of *Paradise Commander*, my first.)

After two years, the little start up college stopped. After another period of unemployment, I worked part time at St Helena parish. The pastor and I split up the work. In most regards, he did everything requiring a priest, and I ran much of the rest with the title of Director, Community Development. That turned out to be my last paid job, lasting six years.

That I now can call myself a published author, I should add, also results from a remarkable confluence of circumstance. Not only was Ronda just down the hall—to become my writing mentor, constructive critic, dear friend of many years, and finally a co-author of three of our books. But it turned out that my first publisher-to-be was in that same early writers' group! Coincidence? I think not. Life has taught me what Jeannie so often said. "God has a plan. God has a plan for everyone."

As any autobiography ought, I have pretty-well identified who I am; or more accurately, who I was and have become under obedience to Transcendent guidance. In sequence: radar systems engineer; radar development program manager; blue water sailor, spouse and father; space operations officer, station commander, strategic planner; catechist, retreat master, spiritual director; college instructor and dean; director of parish community development; published author and most recently, host of a Catholic philosophy discussion panel populated by Ph.D. professors associated with Holy Apostles College and Seminary.

With that list, one would think I never could hold a job! (Maybe I should add to the list pseudo-bum and homeless person?) Never give up! It's never too late!

XV

The Narrow Gate – To the Mountain of God

Go within his gates, giving thanks. Enter his courts with songs of praise. Give thanks to him and bless his name. Who shall climb the mountain of the Lord? Who shall stand in his holy place?

From Psalm 24

Enter through the Narrow Gate; for the gate is wide and the road easy that leads to destruction; and there are many who take it. For the gate is narrow and the road is hard that leads to life, and there are few who find it.

Mt 7: 13

I was sixteen, sitting in a high school algebra II class. Suddenly, my father appeared in the doorway. This, I thought, cannot be good. It wasn't. My maternal grandfather had died, and we were off to Hazlehurst, MS. Sixteen. I was close to "Pawpee," and he was gone. For the first time in my life, I was confronted with the fact of death. His now, and someday, mine. Death became a central issue in my habitual thinking. I was agnostic and afraid. Oblivion, somewhere dead ahead.

At nineteen, I set the whole issue aside. I thought, "I am too young to worry about death. I won't worry anymore until I am old; say, thirty!" Sure enough, thirty showed up way too soon, and I remembered my decision taken at nineteen. By the time we reached Alaska and an older age 33, that fear was popping up almost daily. That was the background to the deep depression I felt during the long 23-hour nights of winter darkness at Clear AFS and Fairbanks. That led to my somewhat desperate "Is there anybody up there?" prayer of January '74, chapter VIII.

The joyous answer came several years later, accompanied by beaucoup mystical and miraculous experiences. (Chapter IX and following.) Eternal life in the offing. *Death, where is thy sting?*

But somewhere in those early years of Faith, a new worry cropped up. Somewhere, sometime in my early Scripture readings I ran into Matthew 7:13, quoted at the head of this chapter. *Enter through the narrow gate.*

I had no clue. What did this mean; what and where was the narrow gate? How do I find it? Fellow Catholics at Patrick AFB, chapter X and XI, had no answer. Finally, I stopped asking; realized that none of them had ever considered Matthew 7:13. But it worried me. I did not want to have come so far and still miss the gate.

Periodically, that question haunted me for years. I knew it was a metaphor, but that did not answer the question. Nor did I find it in my year of formal Scripture studies at Seattle U. Nor in my avocational work as a scripture teacher and retreat master. Nor in my studies devoted to the art of spiritual direction. (Chapters XI and XII.)

Finally, in my practice of spiritual direction, in defining the process for others, the road to holiness, the light lit. The answer was there all along. It had been expressed over and over in studies, readings and masses since my conversion. But not in the same language. And yes, indeed; together, Jeannie and I had found and entered the narrow gate without realizing it.

This, following, is what I have come to realize from a coign of vantage—a more advantageous position in time.

Enter through the narrow gate.... The hard part is finding the gate; recognizing it. It is completely obscured by the weeds and vines of sin. The word "sin" has fallen on many a deaf ear these days, but call it what you will, the effects are real; capital sins are an offense against God's commandments. If not recognized and repented, they lead to life's disasters.

Capital sins are like tall weeds and short weeds and briars and vines: false pride and covetousness and lust and anger and gluttony and envy and spiritual sloth; each with many personal variations. Each can develop into choking domination of one's life; obscuring the narrow gate. They cause us to turn in on ourselves in self-righteousness, self-pity, anger, resentment and addiction to self-destructive habits. They lead toward death of soul.

In this, most theologians and psychologists and philosophers seem to agree. Everyone comes equipped with or soon acquires the seeds of one or more capital sins. The theologian blames original sin. And among the most common and obstructive are the choking vines of self-aggrandizement in quest of wealth, power and the easy life for ones' self. Wealth, power and the easy life are the temptations of Christ in the desert; their roots were revealed among kindergarten four-year-olds (Chapter I), the war over crayon bits.

This is original sin in action: that in infancy, we only demand our own wants and needs. Natural enough, but thereby, life begins in self-absorption. Life must become a school promoting selfless, loving service to others. Many fail the test of servanthood, the test of charity.

Christ rejected wealth, power and the easy life; his temptations in the desert.

Today's culture promotes them. It's not promoting one's own welfare that offends, but an accompanying attitude of disinterest in the welfare of others: the Scrooge approach to life. Rather, detach from obsessive grasping for the temptations of Christ in the desert and promote the good of others through loving-kindness.

Accumulating power or wealth, even the easy life, is acceptable *if* your attitude and works of service willingly are focused on generous serving of others in their need <u>as the primary focus of your life</u>; a life of unconditional love. This is the meaning of *"He who loses his life for my sake, shall find it."* Life must not be so much about having as it is about giving from one's selflessness. But we are not born selfless.

He who would be the greatest in the Kingdom of God shall be the servant of all. That is the essence of love: servanthood expressed through loving kindness. It has to be developed strongly enough to overcome unbridled self-gratification. *....for the gate is wide and the road is easy that leads to destruction, and there are many who take it.*

To enter the narrow gate, you have to clear away the weeds of sin. How to do this? Even my non-practicing protestant mother knew the first step. She used to say, "First, name the beast."

First, name your principle sin(s); identify the weeds of sin that obstruct your selflessness. You cannot pull up, stack and burn the weeds you don't recognize. My mother did the best she could by herself. She did not understand that help was at hand. She did not know to seek a repeating cycle of holy confession, absolution, and grace; the weed eradicating machinery of God as practiced and received in Christ's own Catholic Church.

The great challenge, then, is to persevere in charity when in today's culture there are so many sin-inviting distractions: TV programs and advertisements that con-stantly promote self-indulgence, greed and the easy life; vicarious sports addictions; constant pressures to increase production at work at the expense of reflective time and a multitude of commercial entertainments designed to capture your attention.

And yet, still you must persevere.

Listen to me, ye who live in the senses
And think through the senses only:
Immortality is not a gift,
Immortality is an achievement;
And only those who strive mightily
Shall achieve it.
Edgar Lee Masters (1868-1950) American
Poet, *The Village Atheist (1915)*

The best aid to perseverance I have found is to get rid of the TV and stay out of movie houses. TV, movies and professional football have become the modern-day *Circus Maximus*. There is more to life without TV!

I remember life without TV. We were not assaulted by a constant barrage of suggestive free and easy sex without commitment and responsibility, of gratuitous violence and all manners of lustful self-aggrandizement. Life was more peaceful. There was time for reflection and contemplation. But now there is a subliminal lust for sex, violence and possessions in our society. We cling to news reports of the latest acts of sex or violence, especially among public figures.

Get rid of that tabernacle of the devil – as Father Groeschel calls it! Get rid of that damn TV! And control your use of the internet.

For the gate is narrow and the road is hard that leads to life.

+

Should you clear away your personal sins sufficiently, you will find the narrow gate. Its name is charity; its name is selfless, unyielding, unconditional love. It is unlocked; but hard, still, to open. Its two hinges are corroded from neglect, for... *there are few who find it.*

The lower hinge is called humility. It is freed with the oil of humility. Not the church doormat type, but that humility expressed by living within one's realistic capacities and limitations. One's true condition. Neither to seek and grasp beyond your limitations, nor to waste your real capacities on distractions or sloth. (This does not forbid the realistic increase of your capacities through study, work and contemplation. As the Army slogan says, "Be all that you can be!") Attain self-knowledge and live within the assessment of who you really are. Authentic humility is the basis of all virtue.

A personal example: My parents and teachers encouraged me to pursue a Ph.D. Especially, my mother wanted me to live out her unrealized dream; to become a professor. At twenty-three, the head of the psychology department at Baylor U. offered me a student teaching position and a scholarship to go directly from a B.S. to a Ph.D. We both knew I could succeed. Instead, I pursued a master's degree in management, another in pastoral ministry and a diploma in Spiritual Direction.

Why pass up the Ph.D.? Because I knew myself. I am a generalist, not a specialist. Rather than work at great depth in one or two fields, my gift is a capacity to integrate across a multitude of specialty fields, to coordinate and achieve goals beyond individual capacities. I am at my best as a commander, manager and now, a spiritual director. Know your limits and capacities.

The upper hinge of the narrow gate is obedience; also, a term misunderstood by many. Required is that oil of obedience in deference to legitimate authority properly exercised. Be willing, cooperating, dedicated in obedience. First of all, obedience to God.

They who have my commandments and keep them are those who love me; and those who love me will be loved by my Father, and I will love them and reveal myself to them.

John 14:21 NRSV

Yes, with consistent, holy obedience, God may reveal himself to you.

With the oils of humility and obedience, the narrow gate called unconditional charity opens onto the mountain road of holiness. The road is ever upward, steeper as you go through rocks of latent sin, persecution and unhelpful habits. Persevere.

You will find a few fellow travelers on the steep, rocky mountain road ahead; a few will be following. You will fall and they will fall, and aiding one another, those who persevere will get back on the path and climb ever higher on the mountain of God with the help of that repeating holy cycle of confession, absolution, and grace—the cyclic weed eradicating machinery of God. All while persevering in humility, obedience and servanthood to the needs of others. Yes, the Lord may reveal himself to you in due time. You will "see" the Lord and be glad. You will find unending joy.

Let us go rejoicing, to the house of the Lord.

TO KNOW AND NOT TO DO,
IS NOT YET TO KNOW.

XVI

The Unending Joy – Final Yearnings

JOY – A fruit of the Holy Spirit which helps one to serve God cheerfully. St. Thomas says, "Joy is not a virtue distinct from charity, but an act or effect of charity. (Love)

A Catholic Dictionary, Donald Attwater, Gen Ed.

Two clarifications. First, charity is an inclusive term for love in all its altruistic forms, i.e., voluntary, willing, eager servitude; unconditional love at its best. Christ, Himself, expressed this symbolically in the washing of the Apostles feet.

Secondly, joy in this Christian sense is not simply being extra happy or even giddily happy. It is a sustained level of calm, peaceful joy in good times and in bad, even in the face of persecution, torture and martyrdom. St. Lawrence, as an extreme example, joked with his torturers while they were baking him alive. Such joy only can be explained as a grace received from the Holy Spirit, an effect of unconditional charity. St Lawrence actually loved and forgave his torturers.

But a further note on the significance of the washing of feet. In Jesus' time it was the slaves who had that task. They alone would wash the feet of their master. So symbolically, Christ was placing himself as the slave of his Apostles, of his Church, in humility and obedience—the hinges of the narrow gate!

... you who have fled a world corrupted by lust might become sharers of the divine nature. This is reason enough for you to make every effort to undergird your virtue with faith, your discernment with virtue, and your self-control with discernment; this self-control, in turn, should lead to perseverance, and perseverance to piety, and piety to care for your brother, and care

for your brother, to love.

2 Pet 1:4-7

+

Love casts out all fear. My wife died late in July 2015. Alzheimer's. Earlier, on diagnosis, her neurologist forecasted her remaining life at ten to fifteen years. She was gone in four. But upon the diagnosis, she wrote her life testimony for the edification of our children and her siblings. She remained calm and loving, without fear, exercising servanthood within her declining capacity to the end.

At her death, I added commentary addressed to a wider audience, providing information about her last days. I published it as *Saint Jeannie's Shiny Black Shoes.* I do not call her "saint" through any casual or careless thought. She personified selfless charity throughout the 48 years that I knew her. ... *who would be the greatest in the Kingdom of God shall be the servant of all.*

Typical of an Alzheimer's death, she died of starvation and dehydration. Not that she did not want food and water, but her body absolutely refused them. The last 24 hours were a horror. I was there at the end; never want to see that agony in anyone, ever again. Even after the attending hospice nurse said, "She's gone," the body continued to struggle for life, though there was no breath. It took a half hour for the body's last attempt to live.

And yet, during the last week, the hospice ladies became more and more concerned; not with her, but with me. Finally, the day before Jeannie died, the lead woman looked closely at me with a most worried look and said, "Why do you seem so happy?"

There were many human reasons to be sorrowful, but she was right. I was joyful, energized, exultant! The answer I gave that afternoon was totally inadequate. I expressed only a limited understanding, myself. I mentioned the virtue of detachment which enabled me to make the necessary decisions and arrangements with a clear head despite the fact that I was losing my life partner with whom I had been inseparable for 48 years.

I also could have said, "We had met every commitment we had made to God in his expressed will, to our children in their care and education and to one another in chaste, faithful, and undying love. For 37 years we had kept our vow of unconditional <u>obedience</u> and had worked hard, and yes, joyfully, "in the vineyard" to fulfill the specific will of God for us.

And yes, detachment and fulfilled commitment (obedience) are part of the answer, but it goes much farther. Detachment only is collaborating evidence of true joy attained. Another factor was Jeannie's own will. When clearly, she knew she was close to dying, repeatedly, she said to the attending doctor (in my presence) "I just want to see Jesus!" In that regard, I was happy that she was getting her heart's desire. That gave me considerable comfort. But that was happiness, not constant spiritual Joy.

The primary cause of true spiritual joy first of all is the spiritual gift of grace. I did not know to ask for it, but it freely was given, a sign of God's own love for an obedient servant. A sign of God's own <u>charity</u> at a time of our separation according to His will. The gift of <u>sustained joy</u> in good times and bad. It is still with me. It sustains me to know that if only I persevere, as Jeannie now knows, a share in the <u>divine nature</u> is just ahead on the road up the mountain of God.

Indeed, the above underlined sequence of unconditional detachment, obedience, charity and sustained joy is the road to a share in the nature of God, a beginning share in the divine life.

I also said to the hospice lady, "For 48 years, I have stood with a living saint. What's not to like?"

St. Thomas says, "Joy is... an act or effect of charity. Sustained charity leads to constant joy, a share in the authentic image and likeness of God.

When you are feeling only your losses, then everything around you speak of them...the trees, the flowers, the clouds, the hills and valleys, they will reflect your sadness. They all become mourners...the winds whisper her name, the branches, heavy with leaves, weep for her...but as you keep walking forward with someone at your side, opening your heart, the mysterious truth that your friends death was not just the end but also a new beginning, not just the cruelty of fate, but the necessary way to freedom, not just an ugly and gruesome destruction, but a suffering leading to glory, then you gradually discern a new song sounding through creation, and going home corresponds to the deepest desire of your heart.

Henri Nouwen
Love casts out all fear.

"May you find life with abundant joy in the body of Christ." Al and Jeannie Hughes

Epilogue

Through fear, I learned to ask,
Through asking, I received Answer.
Through Answer, I learned obedience.
Through obedience I understood sin.
Through understanding sin, I learned
empathy.
Through empathy, I learned charity.

Through charity in all its forms, I found joy.

Through joy, I am swept into a share
Of the Divine Life. Amen, and Amen.

Psalm 40

¹ I waited patiently for the LORD;
he inclined to me and heard my cry.
² He drew me up from the desolate pit,
out of the miry bog,
and set my feet upon a rock,
making my steps secure.
³ He put a new song in my mouth,
a song of praise to our God.

Albert E. Hughes

Many will see and fear,
and put their trust in the LORD.
4 Happy are those who make
the LORD their trust,
who do not turn to the proud,
to those who go astray after false gods.
5 You have multiplied, O LORD my God,
your wondrous deeds and your thoughts
toward us;
none can compare with you.
Were I to proclaim and tell of them,
they would be more than can be counted.
6 Sacrifice and offering you do not desire,
but you have given me an open ear.
Burnt offering and sin offering
you have not required.
7 Then I said, "Here I am;
in the scroll of the book it is written of
me.
8 I delight to do your will, O my God;
your law is within my heart."
9 I have told the glad news of deliverance
in the great congregation;
see, I have not restrained my lips,
as you know, O LORD.

¹⁰ I have not hidden your saving help within
my heart,
I have spoken of your faithfulness and
your salvation;
I have not concealed your steadfast love
and your faithfulness
from the great congregation.
¹¹ Do not, O LORD, withhold
your mercy from me;
let your steadfast love and your faithfulness
keep me safe forever.
¹² For evils have encompassed me
without number;
my iniquities have overtaken me,
until I cannot see;
they are more than the hairs of my head,
and my heart fails me.
¹³ Be pleased, O LORD, to deliver me;
O LORD, make haste to help me.
¹⁴ Let all those be put to shame and
confusion
who seek to snatch away my life;
let those be turned back and brought to
dishonor
who desire my hurt.

¹⁵ Let those be appalled because of their
shame
who say to me, "Aha, Aha!"
¹⁶ But may all who seek you
rejoice and be glad in you;
may those who love your salvation
say continually, "Great is the LORD!"
¹⁷ As for me, I am poor and needy,
but the Lord takes thought for me.
You are my help and my deliverer;
do not delay, O my God.

About the Author

Lt. Colonel Hughes (USAF retired) holds an M.S. (with distinction) in Systems Management from the Air Force Institute of Technology, an M.P.M. in Pastoral Ministry from Seattle University (Jesuit) and a Certificate in Spiritual Direction. He taught adults for 25 years as a Catholic catechist and retreat master and has published half a dozen books in the area of spiritual discovery along the road to holiness. He continues to be active as a master spiritual director.

Books by Albert Hughes

- *Paradise Commander* (Corpus Christi, Texas: Good Books Media, 2012)
- *St. Jeannie's Shiny Black Shoes* - my deceased wife's life testimony (Corpus Christi, Texas: Good Books Media, 2015)

- *Buddy, Can you Spare a "Digm" – Confronting the Apocalypse of Indifference* (Corpus Christi, Texas: Good Books Media, 2016)
- *Ice Fog, Spirit Fire, and the Narrow Gate* – autobiography – (St. Louis, MO: En Route Books and Media, 2019)

Co-Authored by Albert Hughes and Ronda Chervin

- *Escaping Anxiety along the Road to Spiritual Joy* (St. Louis, MO: En Route Books and Media, 2017)

- *Simple Holiness: A Six-Week Walk on the Mountain of God* (St. Louis, MO: En Route Books and Media, 2018)

- *What Now?: A Road Map for 80-Year-Olds* (St. Louis, MO: En Route Books and Media, 2019)

Made in the USA
Columbia, SC
11 February 2022

55333291R00129